What's Gone Wrong With the Harvest?

To Tim —
Hope there is an idea
or two here that help.

Jim Engel

Contemporary Evangelical Perspectives Series

What's Gone Wrong With the Harvest?

A Communication Strategy for The Church and World Evangelism

JAMES F. ENGEL & WILBERT NORTON

ZONDERVAN
PUBLISHING HOUSE
OF THE ZONDERVAN CORPORATION
GRAND RAPIDS, MICHIGAN 49506

WHAT'S GONE WRONG WITH THE HARVEST?
Copyright © 1975 by The Zondervan Corporation
Grand Rapids, Michigan

Twelfth printing 1982

Library of Congress Catalog Card Number 75-6174

ISBN 0-310-24161-8

Unless otherwise noted, all Scripture quotations are from the *New American Standard Bible,* copyright 1971 by the Lockman Foundation, and published by Creation House, Inc. Used by permission.

Scripture references from *The Living Bible,* copyright 1971 by Tyndale House Publishers, Inc., used by permission.

Material from *Studies in the Vocabulary* by Kenneth S. Wuest, copyright 1945 by Wm. B. Eerdmans Publishing Company, used by permission.

Material from *Body Life* by Ray C. Stedman, copyright 1972 by Regal Books, used by permission.

Material from *The Church and Its Mission: A Shattering Critique From the Third World* by Orlando E. Costas, copyright 1974 by Tyndale House Publishers Inc., used by permission.

A special word of acknowledgment is given to James L. Johnson whose counsel, example, and inspiration are reflected on every page of this book.

Printed in the United States of America

IN DEDICATION TO

Our wives, Sharon and Colene, who truly are
"worth more than precious gems"
(Proverbs 31:10, Living Bible)
and to the Thursday morning prayer warriors
at Wheaton College,
whose continuous concern and prayer support
made this book possible

Contents

Introduction

In one sense of the word, the Church of Jesus Christ is entering its golden era. Mass media now span the globe, literacy is growing rapidly, people in many quarters are showing new interest in spiritual things. Few now are taken in by the naive philosophy that "things will get better." Quite to the contrary. The world is slowly awakening to the fact that unimpeded materialism and economic growth carry with them the great price of deadly environmental pollution, depletion of natural resources, and debilitating effects on the individual. War, inflation, and the spector of nuclear annihilation are a never-ending threat. What is the answer? Is there any hope?

Into this tempestuous scene Jesus brings the everlasting promise of hope: "Take courage; I have overcome the world" (John 16:33). "If any man is thirsty, let him come to Me and drink" (John 7:37). "God so loved the world, that He gave His only begotten Son, that whoever believes in Him should not perish, but have eternal life" (John 3:16).

Yes, the message of the gospel strikes at the heart of the contemporary scene. Its promise is to bring about *changed lives* and changed social structures. In themselves, education, social reform, and governmental regulation are at best temporary but always fundamentally inadequate answers to the most deeply felt needs of people. More than anything else, mankind needs *"a place to stand"*[1] in a troubled world.

Most people who call themselves members of the Christian

---

[1] A phrase aptly put forth by Elton Trueblood. See *A Place to Stand* (New York: Harper & Row, 1969).

Church would agree with what has been said here. Why, then, haven't we penetrated world society with the fundamental truths of the Good News? There have, of course, been some notable advances, such as dramatic church growth in parts of Africa and South America, but the task of taking the gospel to all nations (all ethnic groups) still is essentially undone.

The great need is to mobilize the resources of the Church of Jesus Christ in a Spirit-led strategy which has as its purpose the fulfillment of the historic missionary mandate of the Church. *The essential task is one of communication.* But communication is more than verbal proclamation. Consider the penetrating words of Orlando Costas:

> We are called in Christ to share with men and women, personally and collectively, the good news of God's king-dom. We are sent to call them to enter into this new order of life through faith in Christ and his gospel. *At the same time,* we are sent to proclaim, in word and deed, the good news of this new order of life *in* the multitudi-nous structures of society — family and government, busi-ness and neighborhood, religion and educations, etc. In doing so, we must stand as Christ did, in solidarity with the poor and the oppressed. Further, we must engage actively in their struggle for life and fulfillment. No dichotomies here: not a vertical vs. a horizontal emphasis of mission; not redemption vs. humanization — but a holistic vision of God's mission to the world and the church's role in it.[2]

While we fully agree with Costas' holistic viewpoint, this book has a more narrow focus on the first aspect of communi-cation — a strategy to reach people in all corners of the world with the Good News and to build them in the faith as they grow to spiritual maturity. In every sense of the word, this book reflects our own pilgrimage as we have grappled with the essentials of a Spirit-led strategy. Obviously this pil-grimage is not finished, and no claim is made here to having found the final and definitive answers. The concepts in the following pages are a distillation of our own experience and

---

[2] Orlando E. Costas, *The Church and Its Mission: A Shattering Critique From the Third World* (Wheaton, Illinois: Tyndale House Publishers, 1974), p. 309.

those of colleagues worldwide who are attempting to utilize contemporary strategies to carry out the work of Christian communication.

The focus of discussion is the local church because it, and it alone, bears responsibility for implementing God's work in the world. The parachurch organization may, for a time, exist alongside the church to perform specialized functions, but its mandate is not a permanent one. What is said in these pages also is highly relevant for the parachurch organization as well, but the church must remain as the distinct focus.

It is necessary to begin with analysis of the situation now existing within the Church. The purpose is not to be negative but rather to uncover fundamental problems and issues so that solutions may be provided. Our intent is not to serve as critics but to be catalysts for change. In many ways we see ourselves represented in the personalities in this book. The lessons to be learned are often the very lessons we ourselves have learned through failure.

This book reflects deep-seated optimism that God's people are undergoing a renewed commitment to fulfillment of those very tasks that have been assigned to the Church. Hopefully, some light will be shed on part of the road that yet lies ahead.

James F. Engel

H. Wilbert Norton

PART I
The Missing Cutting Blades

What's gone wrong with the harvest? Two thousand years ago Jesus faced His followers and said, "Look at the fields — they are ripe and ready for harvest. Go, follow Me, make disciples in all nations." Now, two thousand years later, the fields still remain "ripe for harvest," but the granaries are yet to be filled.

There is no absence of harvesting equipment or potential workers, although it can't be denied that there is much to be done to mobilize and deploy these resources. No, there is plenty of harvesting equipment — churches, powerful radio stations, vast printing facilities, mission boards that span the world. Yet, all too often the *cutting blades are missing* — there is much action but no harvest! The cutting blades of any Christian organization are a *research-based, Spirit-led strategy to reach people with the Good News and to build them in the faith.*

Part I will examine in depth the effectiveness crisis faced by a church that has no cutting blades. First Church of Rollingwood is fictitious in one sense, yet the problems it is facing are those of the church and related parachurch organizations throughout the world. It could just as well be First Church of Osaka or Nairobi or Sao Paulo. While the problems are demanding, there is no cause for pessimism. Later chapters will provide the insights necessary to help restore those missing cutting blades.

1

The Effectiveness Crisis

Tom Bartlett finished his benediction and started down the aisle as the choral amen echoed behind him. *Today is a good day,* he thought, *because the church is packed out except, of course, for the first two rows where no one ever sits out of fear of being seen as "super spiritual."*

Tom had been at First Church for a little over two years now, and when he reached the door and looked back toward the pulpit, he couldn't help feeling some pride at the changes that had taken place. A 33 percent increase in attendance wasn't bad, and the growth at First Church had not gone unnoticed among his friends from seminary days who were having less prosperous years.

"I enjoyed your sermon," said the first person out the door, restraining her three kids who were beginning to express joy at being liberated from their Sunday-morning confinement.

"Thank you, Martha, and how are you and these little guys today?"

"Just fine, Reverend Bartlett, just fine." And so it went. Yes, today was a good day — or was it?

The crowd thinned out and the Bartletts, all six of them, piled into their battle-weary station wagon and headed home. "I think it went well today," Tom exclaimed to his slightly harried wife as she momentarily diverted her attention away from settling that inevitable back seat warfare.

"Maybe so, honey, but what do you think they really mean when they say, 'I enjoyed your sermon'? We hear that week after week, and it sounds like a stuck record to me," his wife remarked. "What do you think they are really saying?"

15

A smothering sensation of doubt rose once again in Tom's heart as he listened to Helen. He knew that most of the compliments on his sermons were sincere. He could preach with the confidence that God had given him a gift as a speaker. Yet, the church seemed to be pretty much the same as it was when he came — larger, but about the same. Was this the kind of Christianity the first-century church experienced?

Monday was Tom's day off and he looked forward to some time on the golf course with Fred Leonard, manager of the Christian radio station in Rollingwood, the suburban community where First Church was located. Fred usually managed to get away from his desk at WTLT (*W*inning *T*he *L*ost *T*oday) for a few hours on Monday morning.

But this week was to be different. At 7:30 Tom received a call from Al Cranston, Chairman of the Board of Deacons at First Church. Al was a charter member of the church which had begun with a group of twelve families in 1961.

"Tom," Al said, "I've got today off because of the strike at the plant, and I think I had better get together with you if you have the time. We just got the results of the congregational analysis last night, and I have some concerns."

Tom fought off a sinking feeling that real trouble might be brewing and replied with a forced sense of cheerfulness, "Okay, Al. Come on over now and we'll take a look at this thing." Deep down, Tom had dreaded the day when this report would come back, because he knew things weren't right at First Church. No matter how hard he tried to escape it, there always was that still small voice saying, "Tom, there is something I have against you." Tom phoned Fred and called off the golf date.

Helen, on her way out the door to face her English classes at the high school, cheerily said, "The coffee's on, honey; praise the Lord that you can have this morning with Al."

Tom didn't feel like praising the Lord, however, because he knew what was coming. For the first time, he was to be faced with inescapable evidence that First Church had dropped to that low common denominator of being a functioning organization, outwardly successful, but inwardly devoid of the sense of the miraculous. Somehow the expectancy born of the conviction that a living God *is* in the world today transforming lives was missing.

In his affable, easygoing manner, Al put down his coffee cup and said, "Tom, I think we are at a crossroads. We face either the greatest opportunity we have ever had, or we can continue as we are, grinding along in a rut. First let's look at the good news. We have 650 members on the books, with an average Sunday attendance of 480. That's up nearly 100 over a year ago. We took in 61 new members last year while we lost 18. Not a bad increase! And the patterns of giving look good too. Most of our people give regularly, and I wouldn't be surprised if about 40 percent tithe. You know that we exceeded last year's budget, and I'm really tickled we are now giving about 33 percent to missions."

Then Al brought in the first sobering note. "Tom, I'm real happy with these figures, but did you know that most of those who joined last year are either transfers from somewhere else or kids from our own family? As far as I can tell, only five people joined who were new Christians. I really don't think that is right, because we should be winning a lot more than that if we are doing our job.

"I'm also concerned, Tom, about the findings from that survey we took of the people during the Sunday service two weeks ago. Here's what it shows. First, 20 percent said they had made some kind of an effort to share their faith with a non-Christian in the past month."

"Wait a minute," Tom interjected. "Two hundred and twenty-five attended the evangelism training institute last fall and I know that a bunch were moving out at least for a while after the training team left."

"I know that," Al replied, "but that was seven months ago, and things have changed. Didn't someone say that sharing is the natural overflow of a Spirit-filled life? It seems to me there just isn't much overflow now.

"Let me go on with this. Thirty percent say they read their Bibles at least three times a week; 21 percent have devotions and prayer with their families; 70 percent don't get together with other Christians except for Sunday morning; 10 percent know what their spiritual gift is and how they can use it; and just a handful seem to be doing something about the social problems of the community. An even more serious problem, Tom, is that almost half claimed they are not being fed spiritually in this church.

"But that's not all. You remember all of the community data we got downtown and from the library? Well, here's what it shows: More than 70 percent of the people here in Rollingwood do not go to church on Sunday and most of those live south of Kennedy Road. Of course, there isn't any church down there — that might help to explain it. Also, there isn't any kind of real outreach to the kids, and the counselors at the high school say they are about at their wits' end with the drug problem. You know, I never realized how far things have slipped in this town, because you just don't find these things out until you pick that rock up and look underneath. Why Police Chief Thompson told me — "

"Just a minute," Tom cut in. "Lay off for a second. Some of this doesn't surprise me too much, because we are just now getting some of our new programs rolling. But that congregational survey! Man, I thought I knew our people better than that!"

Tom asked Al to leave the report so he could look it over, and Al departed after they had a few minutes of prayer together. *These men are concerned,* Tom thought, *because it's obvious something has to be done.* He couldn't help being overwhelmed with a sense of panic. *How can I face them? What's gone wrong?*

THE CRISIS AT FIRST CHURCH

No one can deny it — First Church had lost its cutting blades. When Al Cranston and the others first banded together in 1961, things were different. The Cranstons and the Richards had just moved to Rollingwood. Al and Chuck, the new corporation counsel at the plant where Al worked, soon discovered that they shared something in common — a personal and vital relationship with Jesus Christ. After a few weeks they began to meet together for Bible study, and their small group grew until twelve couples, all living within two miles of each other, found their lives united in a common eternal purpose. The most natural thing to do was to form a new church, since there was no other church that seemed to meet their needs.

Because the Cranstons had the largest home, First Church began there in 1961. For two years, everyone shared in the pastoral duties — and things happened! The joy of this group was contagious and one after another of the neighbors became touched with the presence of the living Christ. Some found Him for the first time. Older Christians discovered that practical Christianity is more than a formal once-a-week activity. First Church grew!

By 1963, it was necessary to move into the grade school on weekends, because the Cranston home had long since become inadequate. It was in that year that the church was formally chartered and called its first pastor, Henry Patterson. Once the constitution was ratified, a more formal organization took over, headed by a Board of Deacons, and six commissions were established to organize the affairs of this growing body. Membership increased, and there still was that undeniable quality of joy, of love, of real community. In retrospect, it was clear that Henry Patterson was the ideal pastor for that time. Although he wasn't great in the pulpit, he had the ability to inspire others and to encourage them to take their rightful place in the Body and to grow in the faith.

Things started leveling off a bit in the early 1970s after the group moved into a new building. The life of the church had been great up to then, especially when everyone was involved in getting that building together. That was just before Tom Bartlett was called to replace Pastor Patterson who had accepted a call to a seminary faculty in another state.

Somehow, something was missing after that. People didn't get together in homes as they once did. Sure, the program was much more organized, and things did work more smoothly. But it seemed as if that early quality of life, that sense of community and vibrant outreach, had been lost. This was the situation Tom Bartlett inherited.

Like many Christian organizations, First Church had progressed through a cycle of effectiveness shown in Figure 1. In the early years of the existence of an organization, it is common for effectiveness to grow very rapidly. In the case of

First Church, effectiveness was clearly evident both in the spiritual life within the Body and in outward witness to the community. Meanwhile, the numbers in the congregation, the budget, the size of the physical plant all continued to grow. Yet these can be misleading measures of success, because all too often they mask an often subtle, yet very real, decline in effectiveness in performing the very purposes for which a group comes into existence. Unless checked, this slump can quickly reach crisis proportions.

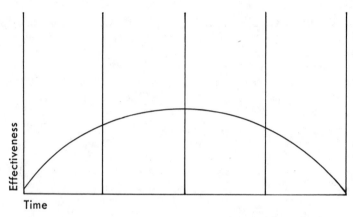

Figure 1. **The Effectiveness Cycle for a Christian Organization**

Yes, First Church was in effectiveness crisis. Tom knew it was happening, and the congregational analysis only confirmed what was becoming obvious. The tragedy is that a church or a parachurch organization may be in a crisis and be unaware of it because of a focus on external measures of success, many of which are irrelevant when viewed from the eternal perspective of a God-given mission.

Tom was right — he had failed thus far. In one sense, he was a product of the system. Four years in one of the best seminaries taught him how to exegete a biblical passage, plumbing the depths of Greek, Hebrew, or even Aramaic. He knew the Bible thoroughly, but he never really learned that biblical content must be related to the felt needs of people if change is to result. In this fundamental sense, Tom escaped the real meaning of communication. Furthermore, he somehow missed the practical significance of ecclesiology in all his theological training. He had never learned how to take his role within a functioning body of Christ, serving in the biblical role of pastor/teacher and shepherd of the flock. The upshot is that Tom had learned mostly how to be a preacher — and this is important — but he had not learned how to be a pastor.

However, the blame was not all Tom's. The membership of First Church also shared the responsibility for effectiveness crisis. In sharp contrast to the early days, they had come to expect "church" to be little more than a Sunday performance by the pastor. They expected to leave "feeling better" and "feeling inspired." But when it came to developing and using spiritual muscle, there was precious little to use. For many, Christianity had come to be just another activity, rather than a pervasive lifestyle characterized by a single-minded purpose to follow the Lord of life and harvest, laying all else aside.

First Church has its Deacons Board. Its role, carefully defined in the constitution, is to govern the church and manage its affairs. Al Cranston in particular saw that the effectiveness slump began about the time that the constitution was ratified. Somehow the biblical pattern of the deacons as spiritual leaders escaped them and responsibility was shifted to one man — the paid pastor.

The constitution further compounded the problem by establishing a formal organizational chart of commissions and committees. Each group has its own task to perform, precisely spelled out. In fact, Cranston had been heard to say in earlier years that "this organizational chart looks better than ours down at the plant." The commissions and committees dutifully meet, carry out their programs, and mostly perpetuate the activities of the past. A spirit of innovation has been replaced by an insidious sense of the routine. After all, why rock the boat when things are going well?

AN ENERGY CRISIS

In short, First Church has come to resemble a secular

organization. First Church, which once was so vital, now is doctrinally orthodox but spiritually sick. It must wrestle with Tozer's prescription for restored effectiveness:

> The Church must have power; she must become formidable, a moral force to be reckoned with, if she would regain her lost position of spiritual ascendancy and make her message the revolutionizing, conquering thing it once was.[1]

---

[1] A. W. Tozer, *Paths to Power* (Philadelphia: Christian Publications, Inc., n.d.), p. 5.

2

Is Anyone Out There Listening?

In recent years the authors have had opportunity to present the concept of the effectiveness cycle (Figure 1) to Christian leaders throughout the world. A common response is, "Did you know that you were describing my situation when you mentioned effectiveness crisis?" Why is effectiveness crisis so commonplace? While there are many surface causes, the root factor is *communication breakdown*. Two particular manifestations of it are examined in this chapter: (1) one-way communication and (2) program orientation.

ONE-WAY COMMUNICATION

Tom Bartlett, like many other pastors, is message-centered. This means that he gives great importance to polishing his sermons, Bible lessons, and other presentations so that there is no question of biblical inaccuracy. This, of course, is commendable and is the characteristic of anyone who is truly concerned with presenting the message of Jesus Christ. Difficulty enters, however, when one places the focus on the message to the virtual disregard of the audience itself.

When pushed to extreme, a message-centered approach will lead to such strategies as door-to-door distribution of Bibles and tracts, or even to contemplation of a worldwide satellite making possible the reading of Bible passages anywhere on the globe. Such strategies can be effective, of course, but there is no guarantee that they will be. One essential question remains unanswered: *What response is there in the lives of the viewers or hearers?*

Much of our effort, then, is only one-way communication — the message is *sent* from the pulpit, over the air, in print, or in person; but the response on the other end is only a secondary consideration. Effective communication, on the other hand, requires that we simultaneously be both message-*and* audience-centered. The person on the other end has full opportunity to ignore us if he wishes. The apostle Paul, as a master communicator, was both message- and audience-centered: "Yes, whatever a person is like, I try to find common ground with him so that he will let me tell him about Christ and let Christ save him" (1 Cor. 9:23 *Living Bible*).

Examine Figure 2 carefully. In cartoon form, it summarizes a wealth of research from linguistics, psychology, and other behavioral sciences.[1] It makes clear that *people see and hear what they want to see and hear,* and this can be devastating to the one-way communicator.

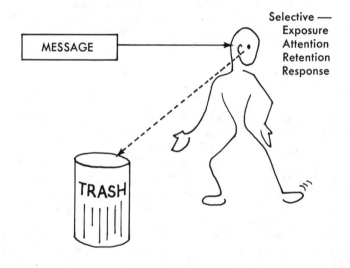

Figure 2. Communication or Chaos?

[1] This evidence is summarized in James F. Engel, David T. Kollat, and Roger D. Blackwell, *Consumer Behavior,* rev. ed. (New York: Holt, Rinehart and Winston, Inc., 1973), ch. 8. The impli-

Notice, first of all, that the message may have *no* effect whatsoever through being avoided, not attended to, miscomprehended, or not retained. Initially the message activates one or more of the senses. We may say, then, that the individual is exposed. Then the message is processed within the central nervous system and the person at this point can exercise a God-given capacity to screen out its content entirely if he so desires.

The point is that God has given each of us a *filter* through which all incoming stimuli are processed. During and immediately after exposure, the filter undertakes a preliminary processing stage in which the message is analyzed and categorized in such terms as pitch, color, etc., largely on the basis of physical properties. But then further analysis takes place — *the analysis for pertinence.* The filter now works to prevent further processing of stimuli that are not seen to be consistent with attitudes, needs, and lifestyle. This is done in several ways. First, the message can be rejected altogether by filtering it out through *selective attention.* It is simply ignored. If attention is attracted anyway, as it often is, the filter then can work through *miscomprehension* or *selective forgetting.*

Assume, for the moment, that you are watching your favorite television program. Does your filter process every commercial that bids for your attention? Obviously not, or we might consider you a candidate for psychoanalysis. On the average, this is what happens: Out of every one hundred people who are actually exposed to a television commercial (they do not leave the room or divert their attention elsewhere),

> Thirty actually attend to its content; i.e., they know what is being said;
> Fifteen understand the content (one half of those who attended to it initially);
> and only five retain its content in active memory twenty-four hours later.

This is a graphic illustration of how the human perceptual

cations for communications strategy are treated more thoroughly in James F. Engel, Hugh G. Wales, and Martin R. Warshaw, *Promotional Strategy,* 3rd ed. (Homewood, Illinois: Richard D. Irwin, Inc., 1975), ch. 4.

filter selectively screens incoming information. These kinds of effects are not confined to the commercial world. There are thousands of published and unpublished studies documenting selective screening in all phases of life — politics, education, and business, among others.[2]

It should not be assumed, therefore, that religious communication is immune from selective perception. Since the early 1970s a number of empirical studies by the students and staff at the Billy Graham Graduate Program in Communications at Wheaton College; Daystar Communications, Inc., in Nairobi, Kenya; Tyndale House Publishers; and others document that people also see and hear what they want to see and hear in that arena as well. For example, it was discovered that most of the Bibles distributed to a particular group of people found their way into the trash can. Another organization found to its dismay that no more than 6,500 out of a possible total listening audience of nearly 8,000,000 tuned to its religious programming on FM radio. Finally, this also happens within the church in that large segments within many congregations show the same patterns of unmet needs that proved to be such a shock to Tom Bartlett at Rollingwood First Church.[3]

The Causes of Selective Screening

Selective screening takes place for two fundamental reasons, the first of which is the *noise barrier*. In the developing countries of the world there is an ever-increasing progression of society toward becoming overcommunicative. Attempts to influence the individual come from all sides, and the result is an exceedingly high noise level that any given communicator can penetrate only with difficulty. People must, of necessity, develop defenses against these attempts at persuasion, or the consequences will be future shock —

the distress, both physical and psychological, that arises

---

[2] See the sources in footnote 1.

[3] These have been done as part of the ministry of Indepth Evangelism Associates (IDEA), a ministry of the Latin American Mission, Miami, Florida.

from an overload of the human organism's physical adaptive systems and its decision-making process. Put more simply, future shock is the human response to over-stimulation.[4]

Therefore, it can be quite a task even to attract attention, because the message is simply drowned out. For this reason alone, attention-attracting techniques, such as dramatic graphics, color, sounds, or movement are often resorted to.

Even if the noise barrier is overcome, there is the profound effect of the *change barrier*. God has created the filter to provide a means of protection against unwanted influence. He knew, of course, that this also could be used to screen out His voice, as is documented by frequent biblical reference to unresponsive soil and hardened hearts. Selective attention, miscomprehension, and selective retention, therefore, can result as the individual resists changes in his beliefs.

The filter itself is formed out of the person's attitudes, beliefs, understanding, and personality. The net effect is to create a "map of the world" that profoundly affects both perception and behavior. Change in this map is resisted to the extent to which beliefs and attitudes are strongly held and are seen as providing an effective means of coping with the world. Insofar as these conditions hold, change will be resisted first of all because it often requires a reorientation that can be both painful and traumatic. Furthermore, why change if there is no felt need for change? The filter, therefore, is tightly programmed and it will close and screen out those attempts at influence that are not seen to be pertinent at a given time.

Appeal to Felt Need — the Key to an Open Filter

Tom Bartlett assumed that his preaching and teaching would somehow fall on responsive soil. He did not take that difficult step of understanding the filters of the members of the audience. If he had, the effectiveness crisis might have been averted.

---

[4] Alvin Toffler, *Future Shock* (New York: Random House, 1970), p. 290.

What is the alternative? Much insight can be gained from the parable of the soils (Luke 8:5-15). Christ saw great differences between those who would be receptive to what He had to say and those who would not. Much of the reason for the nonreceptivity of some soil is that the "worries and riches and pleasures of this life" choke out the seed of God's word (Luke 8:14). Put differently, Christ is saying that filters are closed and there is no real response to anything said because of the absence of *felt need*. The existence of felt need implies the existence of an open filter. For one reason or another, the individual's values, attitudes, and beliefs no longer satisfy. He is now in a stage of problem recognition and is receptive to solution.

Tom Bartlett was stunned to find that about 50 percent of his flock claimed to be in real spiritual hunger and that he had been largely unaware of the specific dimensions of this need. He had gone on Sunday after Sunday preaching his polished sermons while his people sat in their pews, largely unfed and, as a result, even hindered rather than helped in their desire to serve God.

We are referring to the spiritually hungry who are not having their hunger satisfied. Tom must face his responsibility and bring the Word of God to bear in its fullness at the points of need in the congregation. This is by no means easy in view of diversity within the membership, but there are some useful steps toward solution that will be discussed in a later chapter.

This is not to advocate a weak, insipid message that merely appeals to present biases and sidesteps the penetrating truth of the Scriptures. But neither can the Word of God be used as a sledgehammer if people are not receptive. The agent of change starts where people are *now* and moves them toward a desired end point within the context of their existing needs, values, and lifestyles. As Ward Goodenough points out in his landmark book, *Cooperation in Change:*

> But, one may ask, isn't it possible to educate people to see things our way? The answer remains the same: *yes, if they are willing to be educated; otherwise no.*[5]

---

[5] Ward H. Goodenough, *Cooperation in Change* (New York: Russell Sage Foundation, 1963), pp. 107, 108.

THE PERIL OF PROGRAM ORIENTATION

Tom Bartlett has a gift for preaching. He also spends much time in prayer as he prepares his sermons and tries to give the message the Spirit directs. But, as we have seen, Tom's problem is that he really doesn't know his people. True, he visits their homes and sees them at church functions, but he sees mostly the veneer, the masks that people wear. Underneath that mask are Christians, born-again people, who have needs, hangups, and real struggles in applying their faith. That is a dimension of his flock that Tom rarely sees. His messages, therefore, are polished and homiletically correct, but they do not communicate as they should! They are not speaking to felt needs and are falling on barren ground all too often.

Each week Tom must make decisions about sermon content. As Drucker points out, effective decisions start with an opinion as to what should be done but the correct decisions cannot be made until opinion is tested against reality.[6] In other words, Tom must be certain that his sermon content speaks to his people where they are and to their needs, in terms they can understand.

When the opinion about what should be done is not tested against reality, the decision-maker is essentially an "armchair theorist" and is guilty of *program orientation*. The result can be a strategy that is a solution to a nonexistent problem. Program orientation is analogous to a business firm's designing a new product in a laboratory and then trying to coerce people to buy it through the exercise of advertising muscle. Although this may at times result in success, the more likely outcome is a sales disaster. A far better approach, the *adaptive orientation* is to begin with a study of the audience and the other elements of the environment to be faced and to adapt the organizational strategy to the realities of the situation to be faced.

The Deacon Board at First Church also contributes to effectiveness crisis by falling victim to program orientation. There is much activity for all ages, but there is seldom any comprehensive effort made to see if the program really is

---

[6] Peter F. Drucker, *The Effective Executive* (New York: Harper & Row, 1966), p. 143.

meeting the spiritual needs of the flock. Usually decisions are passed solely on untested opinion. And once a program is initiated, it rarely if ever is changed, except, of course, in the most minor of details. The result: smoothly running harvest equipment, except that there are no cutting blades.

Fortunately, Tom, Al, and others in leadership had sensed that things were not right, and therefore they authorized the congregational analysis. Pastor Tom genuinely wants to shepherd the flock, but he needs help. The Deacon Board needs help. The church truly is at a crossroads, but there is one major factor in their favor. The people also are concerned that their "walk does not match their talk." The congregational survey showed that members have deeply felt needs and want help in remedying their deficiencies in the areas of prayer, witness, Bible study, family life, etc. They have not, for the most part, closed their hearts to change, and there is strong evidence of a pervasive desire of the congregation to be God's people.

The great danger of program orientation is that it can quench the Spirit of God. For example, all too often the Board first chooses the Sunday school curriculum and then voices the prayer: "God, bless our decision." This is almost like saying, "Here we are, God; catch up with us." An exaggeration? Maybe, but this is the inevitable end of program orientation. It can quickly become man's way and not God's.

First Church is now poised to break out of program orientation and the result could be a revolution! The congregational analysis was a good first step. The leadership must now go through the demanding task of *adapting* all activities to the needs and requirements that were disclosed. This is not going to be easy, but *there is no other way to restore the missing cutting blades.*

In this book, we are endeavoring to provide practical insight into the dimensions of adaptive orientation. The first step is to understand people, and that is the subject of most of the remaining chapters. Later, we will face the issue of adapting message and media to the situation. The goal is to uncover biblical mandates for the church and the means for their fulfillment in a rapidly changing environment.

PART II
Audience Orientation

First Church of Rollingwood epitomizes the circumstances of churches and parachurch organizations throughout the world: an effectiveness slump brought on by one-way communication and by program orientation. Answers must be found to this dilemma if the church is to take its rightful position as the "light of the world."

We have suggested that the key to restoring the missing cutting blades lies in a communication strategy based on an understanding of the audience. The answer is not in further polishing the message, but rather in an adaptation of what is said to the audience, making sure that what is *sent* is actually *grasped* by the recipient.

Some understandably might object that this sounds suspiciously like Madison Avenue and that we have strayed far from our biblical roots. "After all," they may say, "shouldn't we just follow the example of Jesus and forget all this research and strategy stuff?"

It is the purpose of the next two chapters to demonstrate that the adaptive strategy indeed *is* the strategy of Jesus Christ and that it represents the model given for the church to follow throughout the ages. Concern with effectiveness is most emphatically *not* a modern, Western cultural concept. Jesus warned that all are stewards of God's resources and that each of us will be held accountable for performance (Luke 12:35-49). This insistence on accountability is for people of all cultures, and it must be a prime concern if we take God's word seriously.

3

In the Steps of the Master

"What do we do now? He said we should give everything else up and follow Him, and now He's dead. Everything I had built my hopes on is gone!"

"He said He was the truth and the life. And I know He meant it. There was something about Him that made Him different from anybody else I have ever known."

"Do you suppose we could have gotten Him away before the soldiers got ahold of Him? If only we hadn't been so afraid. Even John and Peter, His closest friends, didn't help."

Two of Jesus' followers were deep in sorrow that Sunday morning as they headed out toward Emmaus and talked about the death of their Master. Their high hopes were dashed. What were they to do next?

Then a stranger joined them. "What's wrong with you fellows? There must be something bothering you."

"Don't you know?" replied Cleopas. "Where have you been? The man who said He was the Messiah, Jesus of Nazareth, was killed by our leaders. And He didn't do anything wrong at all. Now we just heard from some women that His body is gone from the tomb. Somebody even said that an angel told them Jesus is alive. We can't make any sense out of this at all."

"Oh you foolish people," replied this stranger. "Don't you realize that all of this is explained in the Scriptures? Let me tell you about it. May I walk with you for awhile?"

The stranger, of course, was Jesus, although these friends didn't recognize Him at first. As they walked until dark, something began to happen in their lives. It was as if scales were being lifted from their eyes. They understood! Yes, now it was clear. *Jesus was alive, just as the Scriptures said He would be!*

"Peter, John, James — everyone — Jesus is alive! We saw Him! We walked with Him! He's alive!"

"Yes, we know. He has really risen! He appeared to Peter, too!"

Oh, how their hearts burst with joy. And then He stood among them. "Don't be afraid. I'm alive — your friend, Jesus. Touch me. See? I'm not a ghost.

"Now do you remember My telling you that everything written about Me by Moses and the prophets and in the Psalms must all come true? Yes, do you understand it now? Do you see that there is salvation for the world, because *I am here?*

"Now, go and take this message of salvation from Jerusalem to all nations (all ethnic groups). You have seen these prophecies come true. You won't be left alone, because I will send the Holy Spirit upon you as My Father promised. Wait for a while, and go when you have received power from Me."

What had happened? Jesus had said all things before, but now they understood. It seemed as if He couldn't penetrate their filters earlier. At times these well-meaning but very human men had been more concerned about who would be greatest in the kingdom. They had been seeing "through a glass darkly," but now Jesus gave them a second touch. Now they saw clearly; now they understood. On the Emmaus road the two followers were in the depths of intense despair. Their hopes were dashed until Jesus spoke to their felt need. "Don't you see? I have conquered. We have won!"

No wonder they couldn't contain their joy. Now they had a new felt need — the need to share with their brothers who also had a deeply felt need to receive Jesus' good news.

Jesus didn't give what we now call the "Great Commission" as just another commandment. Instead, He could truly direct His disciples by saying, "Now your hopes have all been fulfilled. So go, with the very power of God Himself!"

He knew they would have a strong desire to share and that their message would be brought to many who would be responsive. The world mission of the Church really began that

Sunday morning as two men had a fresh encounter with their Master.

THE BIBLICAL PATTERN

One does not need to consult contemporary books to discover the basic principles of communication. Jesus and His followers have provided a compelling example. They always began with a keen understanding of the audience and then adapted the message to the other person without compromising God's Word. The pattern they followed is as pertinent today as it was two thousand years ago.

Understanding the Audience

Jesus completely understood the nature of man (John 2:25). This was abundantly apparent in all He said and did. When He was asked by the Pharisees, "Why do you eat and drink with the tax-gatherers and sinners?" He answered, "It is not those who are well who need a physician, but those who are sick. I have not come to call righteous men but sinners to repentance" (Luke 5:30-32).

Man was created by God to have fellowship with Him, but then something happened. A willful act of disobedience severed this personal relationship, and man no longer could be complete in himself. He could not please God. Man's disobedience has led to the fact that he now is a slave to self-seeking. He has no choice but to remain imprisoned by his sinful ego, unless, of course, he accepts the liberating gift of salvation offered by Jesus Christ.

Man, then, is incomplete. His destiny is to live with a perceptual filter programmed around the "big I." Yet his conscience and the example provided by creation around him give witness, no matter how dim, to the existence of something beyond himself.

He also is created in the image of God. At the very least, this means he has rational capacities. He can be creative, he can solve problems, he can shape his destiny. This, in itself, is a remarkable quality.

Problem solving and coping with the pressures of life are impossible without a memory. Man can learn from experience. Those things that are functional and helpful in goal-attainment become stored and can be used in the future. Attitudes are formed in the process and these provide further dimensions to the "map" of the world. This God-given psychological mechanism of memory and adaptation is a filter that helps man, first, to adapt and behave in a manner consistent with basic strivings and, second, to avoid influences and behavior patterns that are nonadaptive.

At the heart of this filter, of course, is the ego. Attitudes and beliefs become related in a pattern consistent with this self-concept. Change becomes difficult. Therefore, fallen man is constrained to remain a self-seeker both in thoughts and in deeds. When pushed to its ultimate extreme, this constraint expresses itself in all forms of depravity.

Man's need patterns become a central motivator. Some of these are physical, others are psychological. Always there is the centrality of self-seeking. The filter functions to admit those stimuli that are relevant to the self and screens out those that are not.

Adapting to the Audience

The Approach of Jesus. What a rebuke it was when Jesus said, "I have not come to call righteous men but sinners to repentance" (Luke 5:32). Now what did He mean by this? He was saying in effect, "You people think you have all the answers. You are good Scripture-believing zealots who have no needs. You are completely self-sufficient. (If only you knew what fools you are!) So my message will fall on empty ground. Your filters are closed, and you will not even hear My words."

On the other hand, Jesus could say, "There are many of you here who know your need. You realize something real is missing and you are looking for the answer. I have come, dear friends, for you." He was keenly aware that *change will not occur without the presence of felt need.*

Notice that Jesus varied His message continuously. Now, this does not imply for a minute that He distorted the truth He came to give in any way. Not at all! Rather, He adapted His message to the circumstances — to the needs and backgrounds of those He encountered.

How did Jesus know so much about people? He lived, walked, and talked with them and displayed a genuine interest and concern for their welfare. He met people on the streets, on the hillsides, in the fields, at meals, at work in fishing boats, at prayer, at weddings, on the roads. Such observational research energized by the Holy Spirit provided keen insights.

Jesus took the person from the known and familiar to the unknown through use of parables, illustrations from real life, or symbols with which all were familiar. Both the messenger and the message were received because He built a bond of trust by using the vernacular and speaking to the needs of the people.

In the final analysis, Jesus showed His love by this unique audience orientation. Remember the case of the rich young ruler? This man had a need but he confused the issue. He asked what had to be done to have eternal life.

The Lord wisely answered, "Keep My commandments."

"But I have."

"Then sell all you have and give the proceeds to the poor."

This, of course, was the heart of the issue. Jesus began at the point of felt need and moved from there with great insight to the source of the problem. Undoubtedly, this man betrayed his shortcomings by his flowing robes and the rings on his fingers. Jesus took advantage of observational research.

Did Jesus say to the woman at the well, "Repent and be saved"? If He had she would have dismissed Him as one who was sick from the heat. No, He started at the point of physical need.

"Would you like to have living water, water that will never stop flowing?" He asked.

"*Would* I! Of course! Who wouldn't?"

Then Jesus pressed on, probing deeper and deeper until the

truth emerged. The result? New life and joyous, spontaneous sharing with others: "Come and meet the man who told me all about myself."

Finally, Jesus knew that the purpose of communication is to bring about change. He did not indulge in the luxury of focusing on the irrelevant or superficial. The very heart of the gospel is change. Anything short of this is not true Christian evangelism.

The Apostle Paul. What a picture the fiery young Saul must have presented. An orthodox Jew, he outdid everyone else in his zeal to live for God. He was a faithful Jew if there ever was one. So zealous was he, in fact, that he almost single-handedly set out to eliminate Christians from the face of the earth, undoubtedly out of a sincere motive to root out heresy.

Then one day something happened as he superintended another execution. He saw a man, Stephen, whose life was different. Stephen didn't resist his accusers. His face radiated joy! He said, "Forgive them, father." Stephen had joy and peace — the very things Saul lacked.

Saul couldn't forget this. He must have pondered for hours — just what was it about that Christian? Oftentimes a shattering experience such as this can open a filter in such a way that change is inevitable. Saul now realized he was lacking something, and his encounter with the Lord on the Damascus road found him receptive. Saul had a need and he responded when Christ revealed Himself to him.

Notice the change. Saul, now become Paul, was transformed into a great evangelist and leader of men. He, too, followed in the steps of the Master as he set about on his great mission which was to change the world of his day. On Mars Hill, he took note of the circumstances, of the temples and idols, and began his message with an identification with the hearer. "I see you are very religious and here's an altar to the unknown God. Let me tell you about Him!" Those in Corinth were approached differently. And so he traveled about his world, in each place sharing his message effectively and well.

Now, what about his letters to the churches in such cities as Ephesus and Rome? Paul always began with conscientious research. He knew his audiences. He would write, "Word has reached me that — " or "I hear that — " or "Your letter said — ." He never communicated an abstract message. He always knew precisely what the circumstances were and focused the Word of God, inspired by the Holy Spirit, on their point of need. This by no means always represented what the people wanted to hear. At times his research made it clear the message should be an unmistakable and ringing call for repentance and behavioral change. No doubt there was resistance to what he said. But there also were times when the Holy Spirit worked to open previously closed filters and brought about conviction.

A PATTERN FOR TODAY

Audience orientation, then, was the approach of Jesus and His followers. Indeed, a careful reading of church history will disclose a myriad of examples when the Church succumbed to effectiveness crisis and change became inevitable. If the institution did not change, then, time after time, a new expression emerged, showing anew the vitality that should characterize God's people.

What principles has God given to avoid effectiveness crisis? The best set of guidelines emerges from the Proverbs. King Solomon observed that "any enterprise is built by wise planning, becomes strong through common sense, and profits wonderfully by keeping abreast of the facts" (Prov. 24:3, 4 *Living Bible*). In more detail (from the *Living Bible*):

1. *Analyze the environment; test opinions by fact.* "It is dangerous and sinful to rush into the unknown" (Prov. 19:3). "A sensible man watches for problems ahead and prepares to meet them" (Prov. 27:12).
2. *Make plans based on this information.* "We should make plans — counting on God to direct us" (Prov. 16:9).
3. *Measure effectiveness.* "Anyone willing to be corrected is on the pathway to life" (Prov. 10:17). "A man who refuses to admit his mistakes can never be successful" (Prov. 28:13).
4. *Analyze results and change plans where necessary.* "It is pleasant to see plans develop. That is why fools refuse

to give them up even when they are wrong" (Prov.
13:19).

One theme that consistently runs throughout the New Testament is that the Holy Spirit works by the renewing of our
mind (see Eph. 4:23; 1 Pet. 1:13; Rom. 12:2). We are
expected to analyze, to collect information, to measure effectiveness — in short, to be effective managers of the resources
God has given us. Unless we undertake this discipline — and
it is the very antithesis of program orientation — we effectively prevent the Holy Spirit from leading us! The ever-
present danger is that "a man may ruin his chances by his
own foolishness and then blame it on the Lord" (Prov. 19:3
Living Bible).

THE ISSUE OF MANIPULATION

Some will immediately protest that the adaptive strategy is
little more than Madison Avenue manipulation. The fear is
frequently voiced that a focus on the audience will give the
communicator an ability to control the mind of the recipient
of the message and somehow circumvent logical thought
patterns.

At times, this type of objection is, in essence, an objection
to the change that almost inevitably accompanies conversion.
"Why do you want to change people?" the evangelist is asked.
The best answer is found in the example of Jesus, whose
stated purpose was to bring change — to set people free. If
the gospel is eternal truth, then change also must be the
objective of every Christian communicator who takes the
Great Commission seriously.

Others err by attributing an undue amount of power to the
communicator. We must not overlook the fact that each individual is sovereign — each of us determines through a filtering
process what persuasive communication we will consider.
There is no method known to man by which the filter can be
circumvented and lasting change brought about.[1]

---

[1] For a review of the evidence on this point, especially the issue
of subliminal persuasion, see James F. Engel, David T. Kollat, and

Why, then, is there so much fear of Madison Avenue? Probably the answer lies in the large numbers of advertising success stories and the natural tendency to attribute some semimagical power to the advertiser. When the facts are examined carefully, they lead to quite a different conclusion. Secular communicators also succeed only if they follow the very principle Jesus and others of New Testament times followed: adaptation of message and media to an understanding of the audience. Those who try a contrary strategy run a dire risk, because nearly 90 percent of all new products introduced each year fail. For example, the makers of a new deodorant, Mennen E, discovered that the product did not survive its national introduction even though $12,000,000 was budgeted for advertising.[2] The apparent reason for their failure was that the advertising stressed a product attribute, the addition of vitamin E, which was not relevant to the consumer. On the other hand, Gilette introduced a new men's hair spray with the theme "The wethead is dead. Long live the Dry Look from Gilette!"[3] In two years this product jumped from a 12.2 percent share of the market to 20 percent, and the product did not even exist prior to 1968. Few men want their hair to look greasy or plastered down and Gilette offered a product that met this need.

Secular experience has amply demonstrated that no amount of advertising, no matter how "persuasive" (assuming that there is no deception — quite an assumption in today's world), will succeed if the program goes against the grain of consumer demand. Most marketing successes begin with a study of the consumer — his needs, interests, and lifestyles — to discover those needs that are not now being met by competitors. Then a complete marketing strategy (considering product, price, distribution, advertising, and selling) is developed and adapted to these demand forces.

By no means are we suggesting that the church naively

Roger D. Blackwell, *Consumer Behavior* (New York: Holt, Rinehart and Winston, 1973), ch. 8.

[2] T. G. N. Chin, "New Product Success and Failures — How to Detect Them in Advance," *Advertising Age* (September 24, 1973), p. 61.

[3] Ibid.

apply what the secular world knows. *In reality, the secular world has discovered and applied the very principles that our Lord Himself used.* The need for the Christian communicator today is to follow the Lord's example, recognizing, of course, that the world is characterized by complexity and change. Thus the adaptive philosophy often requires a formalized approach to planning, complete with audience research and measures of effectiveness. In all probability, the apostle Paul would have used such methods also if he were here today. But the basic task is the same: begin with the audience and focus the Word of God on people so that it speaks to their needs.

4

The Great Commission
in Modern Dress

With this grasp of the biblical principles of communication, we now can seriously focus on the true significance of the historic communication mission of the Church. Has it changed? What does it really mean, especially with the growth of modern media and technology? We are not forgetting about Tom Bartlett and the others at Rollingwood. The discussion here is necessary if solutions to their problems are to be found.

MAKING DISCIPLES OF ALL NATIONS

The motto over the First Church choir loft reads, "Go therefore and make disciples of all the nations (ethné), baptizing them in the name of the Father and the Son and the Holy Spirit, teaching them to observe all that I commanded you" (Matt. 28:19, 20). These, as you know, were the last words of Jesus Christ to His Church and they represent the marching orders that are to be followed until His return.

What does this familiar passage mean, however, to the church of the twentieth century? First, it says to *go*. Many of the members of First Church have been trained in evangelism, but only a handful are actually *going*. Not all have the gift of evangelism, of course, but everyone in the Body of Christ is to perform this role when God-given opportunities arise. It is almost as absurd as if one were to sit in a high-powered car waiting for it to move without turning the ignition key and moving the selection lever to "Drive." God cannot work through His Body if it is merely sitting in the pews.

Next, *"make disciples of all nations."* In this context, the word "disciple" is properly translated as "one who follows the precepts and instructions of another."[1] Jesus, of course, was referring to His own instructions. Thus we are given the privilege of sharing the Good News and persuading people everywhere to become followers of the Master. People are not merely to be exposed to the message but are to be won, whenever possible, for an eternal cause.

The Great Commission is not fulfilled, however, merely by proclaiming the message and exposing another to its claims. The convert is to be *baptized* and *taught* to observe all that Christ has commanded the Church. Thus, becoming a disciple is a *process* continuing over a life span as believers are conformed to the image of Christ (Phil. 1:6). The Church has a definite obligation to cultivate the new believer, helping him or her to grow in the faith.

It appears, then, that the Great Commission contains three related but distinctly different communication mandates: (1) *to proclaim* the message; (2) *to persuade* the unbeliever; and (3) *to cultivate* the believer. Part of the problem with the harvest comes from fuzzy thinking at precisely this point because of a tendency to blur the essential distinctions between these communication functions.

Figure 3 is of critical significance, because it represents an attempt to place these communication ministries in the perspective of the spiritual decision process that is followed as one becomes a believer in Jesus Christ and grows in the faith. This model of spiritual-decision processes in some ways is similar to decision models in other areas of human endeavor.[2] But it represents a vast step beyond mere secular models in that it depicts the interactive role of both God and the human communicator in this process.[3]

---

[1] Kenneth S. Wuest, *Studies in the Vocabulary* (Grand Rapids: Wm. B. Eerdmans Publishing Co., 1945), p. 25.

[2] See, for example, the model of consumer behavior in James F. Engel, David T. Kollat, and Roger D. Blackwell, *Consumer Behavior,* rev. ed. (New York: Holt, Rinehart & Winston, Inc., 1973).

[3] This model as presented here has undergone an interesting history. In rudimentary forms, it was first suggested by Viggo Sogaard while he was a student in the Wheaton Graduate School. It later was revised by James F. Engel and published in such sources

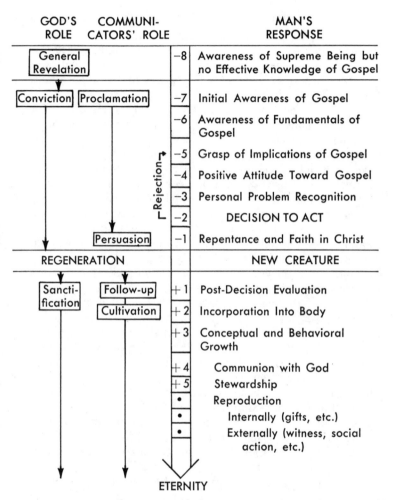

GOD'S ROLE	COMMUNI-CATORS' ROLE		MAN'S RESPONSE
General Revelation		−8	Awareness of Supreme Being but no Effective Knowledge of Gospel
Conviction	Proclamation	−7	Initial Awareness of Gospel
		−6	Awareness of Fundamentals of Gospel
		−5	Grasp of Implications of Gospel
		−4	Positive Attitude Toward Gospel
		−3	Personal Problem Recognition
		−2	DECISION TO ACT
	Persuasion	−1	Repentance and Faith in Christ
REGENERATION			NEW CREATURE
Sancti-fication	Follow-up	+1	Post-Decision Evaluation
	Cultivation	+2	Incorporation Into Body
		+3	Conceptual and Behavioral Growth
		+4	Communion with God
		+5	Stewardship
		•	Reproduction
		•	Internally (gifts, etc.)
		•	Externally (witness, social action, etc.)

(labeled vertically between columns: Rejection)

ETERNITY

Figure 3. The Spiritual-Decision Process

as *Church Growth Bulletin* and elsewhere during 1973. Since that time, modifications have been introduced as others have made suggestions. Particularly helpful comments have been advanced by Richard Senzig of the communications faculty at the Wheaton Graduate School and Professors C. Peter Wagner and Charles Kraft of the Fuller School of World Mission.

Everyone will fall somewhere on the continuum represented in Figure 3. Some will have awareness of the Supreme Being through God's ministry of general revelation (conscience and nature) but no effective awareness of the gospel. Others will have the necessary awareness and grasp of its implications. When this is accompanied by strong felt need for change (designated as personal-problem recognition), the individual is open to a challenge to turn his life over to Christ. Prior to that time, there is neither sufficient understanding nor felt need to permit a valid response to such a challenge. Those who have made such a commitment, then, are in various stages of spiritual growth as they are being conformed to the image of Christ through the ministry of the Holy Spirit.

God and man uniquely interact to influence the spiritual decision process. It is God's sole responsibility to bring about awareness of the Supreme Being through general revelation. The human communicator has no role in this whatsoever. From then on, however, the human communicator assumes a critical responsibility. It is his task to impart the necessary awareness of the claims of the gospel through a ministry of *proclamation* as God, through the Holy Spirit, convicts the recipient of sin. Once sufficient biblical awareness and problem recognition have been achieved, the function of the communicator is to *persuade* — to call for a life commitment to Jesus Christ. After this step has been taken, God, and God alone, imparts new life through regeneration.

New life does not stop, of course, with regeneration. The new life of the new believer must be *followed up* and *cultivated* while God brings about spiritual growth through the ministry of sanctification. Such maturation continues throughout a lifetime for eternity.

Each person's spiritual journey is a lifelong decision process. It may begin many years prior to the point when a decision is made and one becomes born again, or regenerated, in the biblical sense. There usually is a complex of influences in this process and these must be understood.

The responsibility of the Christian communicator is to approach people where they are in terms of their spiritual position and, through an appropriate combination of message and media, to cause them to *progress in their decision process toward initial commitment and subsequent growth.* The goal, in short, is to bring about demonstrable and *measurable* change in people with respect to their response to the gospel.

Proclamation

Often in non-Western countries, the vast majority of the potential audience, 90 percent or more, will be at position -8 on the continuum in Figure 3 and have little or no effective knowledge of the gospel. At the very most, they will have some awareness of God's power through the witness of creation and their conscience as Paul asserts in his letter to the Romans. But this is hardly a sufficient basis for a life-changing decision. A simple presentation of the plan of salvation, often containing little more than a few major propositions backed up by several Scripture references, is likely to make little sense to a person who doesn't even know what the Bible is, let alone its claims about God, the nature of man, and the uniqueness of Jesus. Such a simple gospel presentation will be screened out and ineffective until the person has reached stage -3 accompanied by a grasp of the implications of the Good News and problem recognition.

What is the minimum level of biblical understanding required for one to make a valid life commitment to Jesus Christ? This is a question of enormous significance, and it is likely that there will be some important variations from one cultural grouping to another.[4] But most will agree on three basic categories:

1. a belief in one God,
2. a proper recognition of the biblical significance of the nature of man as a sinner, and

---

[4] The writings of Charles Kraft bring important insights into cultural variations. See, especially "God's Model for Cross-Cultural Communication — the Incarnation," *Evangelical Missions Quarterly,* vol. 9 (Summer, 1973), pp. 205-16; "Dynamic Equivalence Churches: An Ethno-theological Approach to Indigeneity," *Missiology,* vol. 1 (January, 1973), pp. 39-57; and "Christian Conversion As a Dynamic Process," *International Christian Broadcasters Bulletin* (Second Quarter, 1974), pp. 8, 9, 14.

3. a grasp of the uniqueness of Jesus in salvation.

These points will be elaborated in much greater depth in later chapters.

The goal of the communicator is to build awareness in these three categories and to stimulate, if possible, a positive attitude toward the Christian message and toward its visible manifestation, the Church. This is the essence of the ministry of proclamation — stimulation of awareness, initial interest, and positive attitude. More specifically, it brings about movement from -8 to -3. Another word for this type of communication, and an unfortunate one, is "pre-evangelism." This implies that the proclamation is not true evangelism, an unwarranted position from the perspective of the decision process in Figure 3. Anything that stimulates movement from one stage to the next is a vital aspect of successful evangelism, even if it does not culminate in the actual decision at that point.

Persuasion

Most training in evangelistic technique focuses on methods of persuasion — simple, dramatic presentations that provide the essence of the gospel, with special focus on the steps necessary for a decision. Persuasion, therefore, is Christian communication designed to call for and facilitate a life commitment to Jesus Christ.

Persuasion, however, will be inappropriate unless the recipient of the message has reached stage -3 — problem recognition. Problem recognition occurs when the Holy Spirit, by producing conviction, brings about a perceived difference between the actual state of affairs and the ideal state of affairs. This, of course, serves as a powerful motivating force for change, which, in turn, is usually followed by a search for information and high receptivity to *relevant* communication. The filter now is open and responsive and this is the key indicator of "fields ripe for harvest."

What brings about this state of problem recognition? As the next chapter elaborates, there are times when communication content itself can perform this function, but it must be remembered that absence of a recognized problem, and hence of felt need, implies a closed filter. Thus, there are limitations on what man can do with the message and the media.

An all-too-common mistake is to utilize persuasion in such a way that the individual is, in effect, manipulated to make a decision that usually proves to be an abortive one. Visualize the following scene, for example: The preacher has finished his sermon and is about to give the invitation. At his quiet signal the organ softly begins playing and the choir strikes up with "Just As I Am." The preacher exhorts, "Friend, if the Spirit is moving in your heart, come forward now; come forward now and give your life to Jesus. Don't delay, because this may be the last chance you will ever have. That's it; keep coming. You, back there, Jesus is working on you. Come forward, give your heart to Him." And when the trickle of inquirers diminishes, the choir strikes up again, louder this time.

Let it be understood that this type of invitation still is used by God to bring people to repentance. But it also may be used by man to "brainwash" people into coming forward. The combination of soft music and not so subtle exhortation can get people to the front, all right, but what does this action mean? Does it really signify that all-important step of faith that Jesus asks? Unfortunately, there have been too many instances of a recording of so-called "decisions" that were not decisions at all.

What, after all, is the true meaning of a "decision for Jesus Christ"? Does it require that people "pray and invite Jesus to come into their heart"? Many, including the authors, came to Jesus in this way. But is such a prayer necessary? Where *precisely* in the Bible is this strategy of witness suggested or even alluded to? Some immediately will point to Revelation 3:20. A more careful analysis, however, will reveal that God was speaking there to a moribund church and was offering a collective promise of restoration to spiritual power if they would only take the first step of volition and permit Him to resume His role as Lord. It is not primarily a salvation verse!

This may come as a real shock to some readers and the authors can anticipate the waves of response. Some will ask, "After all, didn't you pray such a prayer of invitation?" Yes, but, when it comes right down to it, salvation came *only* upon the kind of belief the apostle Paul talked about in the tenth chapter of Romans — a step of faith in which one rests completely on the assurance that Christ's claims are true and that He *is* the only way. The prayer of invitation or commitment is basically an outward manifestation of such belief, and a helpful one at that, at least in the North American setting. Feeling the need of praying such a prayer gives the inquirer something tangible to do and hence the prayer can be a useful aid in bringing him to salvation. But to make serious reference to Revelation 3:20 and claim that such a prayer is normative is inappropriate, because *saving belief comes by standing on the Word God has spoken.*

All too often, evangelistic campaigns have been judged successful (or not successful) on the basis of how many "prayed." A common occurrence in the evangelical church is to applaud the preacher who gets the most "decisions." Seldom do we ask after a short period of time how many "converts" show real evidence of regeneration, of the fact that "old things have passed away and all things have become new." Some rather surprising things can be discovered if this important inquiry is made.

Hundreds of supposed decisions were reported in an evangelistic campaign in India, but later analysis showed that those who came forward and "prayed" were only expressing interest. Few truly came into saving belief, but the evangelist enthusiastically reported his results to his North American supporters, little realizing how erroneous his evaluation was.

Similarly, a group of Japanese pastors and laymen were trained to share their faith through a strategy of persuasion of this kind, using door-to-door witness. Many apparent decisions resulted but, once again, those who made decisions just seemed to disappear into the woodwork. Why weren't they joining the church as one would expect? Any keen observer of the Japanese scene could quickly supply some answers. First, the use of persuasion at the beginning is usually the wrong strategy because the vast majority of the population have little or no knowledge of Christianity. The real need is for proclamation, followed later by persuasion. Secondly, the cultural norms of courtesy often will lead people to comply simply to avoid offending. Finally, the average person "prays" to many gods, so why not also pray to Jesus "just to make sure"? As Goodenough has said, "Some agents of religious change . . . making assumptions about the universal needs of the soul in keeping with their own values, are notoriously naive about the motives that made converts of their clients."[5]

Again, the purpose here is not to attack any particular evangelistic technique, but rather to avoid a strategy that may be culturally appropriate in some places but inappropriate elsewhere. The examples cited reflect a particularly insidious form of program orientation referred to by the anthropologist as *ethnocentrism*.[6] This is where the one who is trying to bring about change in a culture other than his own imposes his norms and behavior patterns on others. The consequences of ethnocentrism can be catastrophic. More will be said about this later.

The objective of persuasion, then, is something quite different from getting people to come forward or to pray a prayer. The objective is to focus on the reasons why a person is at the stage of problem recognition and to present the biblical solution in a logical manner, in terms appropriate for that individual's felt needs. Thus, the evangelist clearly presents Jesus as the solution to his or her problem and provides concrete steps to bring the inquirer to the point of saving faith. The specific form of these steps, however, must be a *variable* and not a *constant* if the errors of ethnocentrism are to be avoided.

Regeneration

The objective of persuasion is to lead to regeneration, but not every apparent decision will have this result. Some will be brought to the point of decision and draw back from the commitment that is demanded. This is depicted in Figure 3 by an arrow indicating that the communicator must once again stress the fundamentals of the gospel message and its implica-

---

[5] Ward H. Goodenough, *Cooperation in Change* (New York: Russell Sage Foundation, 1963), p. 57.

[6] See ibid., pp. 39-42, for an excellent discussion.

tions. In effect, by refusing to accept Christ, the individual has regressed to stage -5.

Whatever the content of the message, communication can never do more than set the stage for regeneration, which is accomplished only through the Holy Spirit. In Titus 3:5 Paul speaks of the love of God and points out that "He saved us, not on the basis of deeds which we have done in righteousness, but according to His mercy, by the washing of regeneration and renewing by the Holy Spirit." This verse overflows with meaning for the exegete who is directed to world evangelization. One authority puts it like this:

> The act of regeneration made them partakers of the divine nature. This is the basis upon which the Holy Spirit works in the Christian's life. *He has in His hands now an individual who has both the desire and the power to do the will of God. He augments this by His control over the saint when that saint yields to Him and cooperates with Him.* The first is *paliggenesia,* the second, *anakainosis,* the first regeneration, the second, renewing.[7]

Obviously, God and man work together in this mysterious New Testament process. If there has been no proclamation and no persuasion, the communicator has failed to provide that essential level of understanding that the Holy Spirit uses to bring about regeneration. In short, God expects His Body to communicate — to understand the audience, to speak to felt needs, to build awareness.

Cultivation

The decision process does not cease when the believer has become spiritually alive. Rather, the Holy Spirit now undertakes sanctification, which results in a growing conformity over a lifetime to the image of Christ (Rom. 8:29; Phil 1:6).

Notice in Figure 3 that spiritual growth begins with post-decision evaluation (stage +1). This is an inevitable consequence of a major decision in which unchosen options also

---

7 Wuest, *Studies in Vocabulary,* pp. 94, 95.

have some attractive components.[8] The new convert may wonder what he has gotten into, for example, and may enter into a stage of real doubt and confusion. Thus it is always necessary to provide for early follow-up in which teaching relating to assurance of salvation is presented and the basic essentials of Christian growth are explained. Impaired spiritual development or even retarded Christian growth may result if follow-up is neglected.

The next requirement is to incorporate the new believer into the Body of Christ (stage +2), without which there can be no true spiritual maturity. The writer of Hebrews admonishes Christians to "consider how to stimulate one another to love and good deeds, not forsaking our own assembling together, as is the habit of some but encouraging one another" (Heb. 10:24, 25). While there are doctrinal differences on this point, formal incorporation into the Body is often accompanied by the act of baptism, signifying the convert's forsaking of the past and desire to serve God with his full volition.

Now the Christian life begins in earnest. There will be within the Body some immature new believers at stage +3. Others will show greater maturity (stage +4 and beyond) and will have different needs. All, however, are in the *process* of conformity to the image of Christ. There is no such thing as reaching a final point of maturity — in this lifetime, at least.

Each believer must show conceptual understanding and behavioral growth in at least three foundational areas:

1. communion with God — through personal and corporate prayer and worship
2. stewardship — the continuing commitment of all aspects of one's being to God and the use of these resources in His service
3. reproduction — ministry to others and thereby a reproducing of the power and love of God in them
   a. internally, within the Body of Christ through use of spiritual gifts
   b. externally, to the world through verbal witness, social concern, etc.

---

[8] For a review of the literature on this phenomenon, see Engel, Kollat, and Blackwell, *Consumer Behavior,* ch. 22.

The foundation of spiritual growth is conceptual: knowledge of the Word of God. For this reason, the ministry of teaching rightly assumes a primary place in the Church. But what represents good teaching? Is it merely the planting of biblical doctrine in the "frontal lobe," as one well-known Bible teacher has widely asserted? Some would respond affirmatively and assert that the amount of doctrinal knowledge one has is the best gauge of his spiritual maturity. On this assumption, the new believer thus would be cultivated primarily through straightforward doctrinal teaching and preaching.

If doctrinal knowledge itself is the essence of spiritual maturity, however, then the evangelical church, especially in the United States, should be characterized by believers who are using their spiritual muscle to "turn the world upside down." There would be a continual frontal attack on the ills of society, and church members would be joyfully witnessing to the power of the risen Savior as did their first-century counterparts.

Unfortunately, the evangelical church tends to be characterized more by spiritual impotence than by spiritual muscle. First Church in Rollingwood and its well-meaning body of believers could represent a church in any community in the United States, as well as in many foreign countries, where Christianity has lost its cutting edge and faces effectiveness crisis. If doctrinal knowledge itself is sufficient to keep the cutting blades sharp and operative, Tom Bartlett would not be facing his dilemma. In one sense, the people of First Church have been well-taught during most of their spiritual lives, but apparently something essential is missing.

Tom Bartlett does not really understand the spiritual-growth process. Once again, this is not completely his fault, since he was taught in his professional training to be a preacher rather than a pastor. Tom is now beginning to see that the key to growth and fruitfulness in the life of the Christian comes in the struggle to *apply biblical teaching* to the problems of everyday life. The congregational analysis shocked him into the awareness that his members, under their spiritual masks, are having some deep struggles in arriving at a lifestyle that conforms to the example Jesus gave.

In reality, the existence of these problems and struggles is a positive sign that believers are taking their Christianity seriously. Their absence, on the other hand, implies an almost Pharisaical existence in which the believer has "arrived" at a comfortable, satisfying life that is outwardly Christian and orthodox but inwardly void of anything approaching Jesus' standards. It is the "broad, easy way" in contrast to the narrow, twisting way.

The facts of man's created nature indicate that initial and continued growth and fruitfulness involves a progression of decisions initiated by problem-recognition and followed by a struggle to find the correct way. This is a natural but tortuous process in which the believer is conformed by the Holy Spirit to the image of Christ. The Spirit initiates felt need by showing the gap that exists between "what is and what ought to be." The believer, then, must decide what to do — either to *obey* under the guidance of the Spirit and appropriate God's solutions or to *disobey* and, in effect, slump into a stage of arrested growth.

The point is that the believer must be helped in this struggle. This is the true meaning of cultivation. At times it will be necessary to prune and admonish. At other times the need is for fertilization — encouragement, guidance, and teaching.

Tom Bartlett did not really know the members of his congregation in the terms most critical for his ministry. He saw only the exterior and hence was unable to do much more than impart doctrine that was largely *devoid of application*. It is no wonder that First Church faces its dilemma. If Christians aren't receiving solid guidance in applying biblical truth to life, the church or the parachurch organization is failing in cultivation.

Spiritual reproduction becomes virtually impossible if the believer's spiritual growth is arrested either because of disobedience or because of inability to find satisfying answers to personal problems in his spiritual pilgrimage. There is little reproduction within First Church or beyond its walls. Life in that congregation certainly is not characterized by the element of the "miraculous," which always will be present when the Body of Christ is truly alive and functioning under the control of its Head.

It is not intended here to place the blame entirely on Tom

Bartlett, but he is, after all, the shepherd of the flock. Accountability for the life of First Church resides with him. Obviously, he can begin remedial action by adapting his teaching and preaching ministry to the issues raised by the congregational analysis. Much more than this will be required, however, because First Church must consider once again what the biblical model is for a functioning Body.

THE IMPORTANCE OF MEASURABLE GOALS AND CHURCH GROWTH

It has been repeatedly stressed that the intent of Christian communication is to bring about change! This also is the basic thesis of church-growth theory. Because of the importance of church-growth concepts, no discussion of the requirements of the Great Commission is complete without an analysis of these precepts.

The church-growth thesis is a simple one: The goal of any program of evangelism is to produce disciples. If disciples, therefore, are being produced, the outward manifestation will be measurable numerical growth within the Church.[9] Making disciples is defined in terms of the numbers of those who accept Christ, show evidence of regeneration, and are incorporated into the Body of Christ. The proclamation and cultivation ministry of the Church has received less emphasis in this context, at least according to the published writings on the subject.

The church-growth model obviously encompasses the persuasion ministry and is appropriate only when people have reached stage -3 in Figure 3. Prior to that time, there is not sufficient understanding and felt need to permit much reaping in terms of lasting life commitment, and the fields are judged to be green and immature for purposes of evangelism. Advocates of church growth concentrate on ripe fields, therefore, and mount an aggressive strategy of persuasion to

---

[9] See C. Peter Wagner, *Frontiers in Missionary Strategy* (Chicago: Moody Press, 1971); and the various writings by Donald A. McGavran, especially *Understanding Church Growth* (Grand Rapids: Wm. B. Eerdmans Publishing Co., 1970).

achieve measurable growth in numbers on the church rolls. The ministry is to take individuals through the stage of incorporation into the body (stage $+2$).

The emphasis on church growth has produced salutary effects in many parts of the world, but the discerning reader will quickly grasp that the church-growth model is not applicable to every situation. For example, most people in the country of Japan fall at -8 on the continuum and aggressive persuasion is clearly out of the question until sufficient proclamation has been undertaken to bring large numbers to stage -3. Much of Catholic South America, on the other hand, is presently characterized by sufficient numbers at stage -3 to warrant the church-growth emphasis. Indeed, a failure to produce church growth in such ripe fields is nothing more than a clear sign of an inactive and even moribund church.

If the fields are not ripe, however, utilization of the church-growth model can have some adverse effects:

1. It is probable that relatively few will become converts.
2. The conclusion may be reached that people are not open for evangelism at this time and that efforts ought to be concentrated elsewhere. This would be an erroneous conclusion, however, because the strategy is wrong. *The stress should be on proclamation and not on persuasion.*
3. A strategy of evangelistic proclamation may be minimized or avoided altogether as resources are shifted toward those fields or audience segments where there is evidence of greater problem recognition. The net result, of course, would be that nothing is done to help these people advance in their decision processes.

Let it be noted again that the church-growth model is explicitly designed for use only when there is evidence of widespread problem recognition. For this reason, the various writings place heavy emphasis on discovering fields that are "ripe for harvest" and concentrating resources there.

Church-growth advocates have rightfully stressed the importance of numerical, measurable goals. Numbers added to church rolls, of course, are not difficult to measure. The results of proclamation and cultivation, however, present some measurement problems. In fact, Wagner argues that some have been proclaiming for too long without any discernible results.[10] If reference is made only to numbers of converts, such a criticism is not valid, because the results of proclamation can be detected *only* in terms of shifts in awareness and attitude. Such shifts, in turn, *are* measurable by using known methods.[11]

While measurement is the subject of later chapters, it should be stressed once again in broad terms that successful communication moves people in their decision processes (Figure 3). Success does not require a prayer of commitment, but it does require discernible movement. If this does not occur, it may be a sign that people in an audience segment for some reason cannot be reached with the gospel or that the methods used are inappropriate.

---

[10] Wagner, *Frontiers in Missionary Strategy.*

[11] See James F. Engel, Hugh G. Wales, and Martin R. Warshaw, *Promotional Strategy,* 3rd ed. (Homewood, Ill.: Richard D. Irwin, Inc., 1975), ch. 9.

PART III

Proclamation, Persuasion, and Cultivation: Toward Restoring the Cutting Blades

Now, with this overview of biblical communication principles and the task of the Great Commission behind us, it is time to return once again to the community of Rollingwood. First Church, of course, is seeing only minimum results in proclamation, persuasion, and cultivation; and the reasons for this have been made clear. What can now be done to reverse the slump in effectiveness? This is the important question of the next four chapters.

George and Sally Calderone now enter the picture. They are two typical residents of Rollingwood and are about to make the greatest discovery of their lives, that of knowing Jesus Christ personally. From their experience we can grasp something of the nature of the spiritual decision process that could be discussed only in the most general terms in chapter 4. Chapter 5 discusses how the initial encounter with Christ took place in this family and chapter 6 focuses on the implications for the strategy of proclamation and persuasion for First Church and other churches in Rollingwood. Chapter 7 returns to George and Sally once again as they struggle to grow in their new-found faith. Chapter 8 takes the broader perspective of the implications for the strategy of cultivation.

George and Sally's experience obviously is not normative and no attempt is made to claim that it can be generalized. Everyone comes to a relationship with Christ in a different way. But there are some commonalities, and generalizations can be made from that standpoint. George and Sally are introduced to avoid the sterility of a broad, general overview, and much can be learned in this way.

5

Freedom!

It was a typical morning at the Calderone household. Everyone was too rushed at the breakfast table to do anything more than grunt at each other and rush off into his or her own little world. As George finished his coffee, he couldn't help wondering what life really was all about. What a rat race! And Sally had exactly the same thought.

The Calderones had moved to the Kennedy Road area in Rollingwood just a few months before, and their home certainly was one of the most attractive in the community. George had done well as advertising manager at the Ace Bakery, and, from the exterior at least, the Calderones appeared to be an ideal, all-American family. What the world couldn't see, however, was the extent to which George and Sally's marriage had gone sour. They seemed to be living in a state of "armed truce," not really close to a parting of the ways but at a point where each simply tolerated the other.

Everything should have gotten better when they moved into the new home. This was Sally's great dream, to have that "all-electric kitchen" and the latest of everything. But life didn't really change. The circumstances were different but the emptiness remained.

George had climbed most of those mountains which had been set before him. At thirty-four years of age, he had gone nearly to the top at the plant, and many were saying that he was next in line for Al Cranston's job as general manager. But what would that promotion really mean? Probably only more work. Money no longer provided the motivation it did, and George had come to the point where climbing another mountain just didn't provide the same sense of challenge. Every time he reached the top, there just seemed to be another mountain ahead. Where would it all end?

One of George's real joys was to get behind the wheel of his Mercedes. Turning out of the driveway that morning, he was relieved to get away from the noise and tension of life for a few minutes. But the thought of heading for the office only brought a new set of tensions. *If things don't ease up,* he thought, *they'll be wheeling me into the emergency room one of these days. Maybe there's some good music on the radio.* As the sound of FM stereo boomed throughout his car, George was jolted by a harsh voice that seemed to scream, "Sinner, you will only go one place if you don't accept Jesus, and that is to hell. Friend, you need Jesus now! Repent and turn to him."

George had accidentally turned to WTLT, the Christian radio station. He swore aloud. "That's all I need this morning," he grouched, as he spun the dial over to the "wall-to-wall" music station he usually listened to.

George had gone to church as a child. After all, that was the thing everybody did. He met Sally there and later married her, and that was just a normal part of his life. He and Sally soon dropped out of church, however, as the excitement of being newly married squeezed out spiritual realities. Both had come to the opinion that most churchgoers were faced with the same hangups they were beginning to experience. Why go there to hear answers given to questions they weren't even asking?

The kids still attended Sunday school, of course, but George and Sally had been seriously considering giving in to their incessant demands to let them drop out, too. "Dad, if you and mom don't go, why should we?"

Sally and George were pretty well turned off on the church. A few months earlier they had been called on by a couple from First Church who came to the door on a community survey. They were willing to talk that evening and the callers stayed quite a while. But somehow communication never really took place. The church callers wanted to talk a lot about a little booklet that showed the "steps to God," but they just evaded the deep questions George raised. When they left, they said they would come back again. But they never did. George had been through it all before. "If we don't give the answers they want," he told Sally, "they just write us off. First Church is just like all the others — they really don't give a hang about us." No wonder the preacher on WTLT that morning only served to turn him off even more.

When George arrived at the office, what he found there made him want to leave it all and head back home. The production manager was waiting for him with the news that production had to be cut back at least 40 percent because of a shortage of sugar and boxes. But the advertising George had worked on so hard was already underway. What was he to do? Contracts had been signed for space and time, and the new commercials were playing.

Al Cranston knew the moment he saw George at the coffee urn that the lid was about to blow. Al, as you will remember, was chairman of the Board of Deacons at First Church as well as general manager at the bakery.

"George," Al said, "I know the mess this shortage thing has put you in, but we've got no choice but to cut back."

"It isn't only that, Al," George replied. "It just seems as if this has come on top of everything else."

"I'll tell you what," Al suggested. "Why don't you join Chuck Richards and me for lunch today. We usually get together once a week just to share our problems and our joys. We'd be tickled to have you."

That day was to launch George Calderone on the way to freedom — freedom from slavery to himself. George had always seen something different in Al and Chuck. He knew they took their religion seriously. They didn't seem to wear it on their sleeves, but it did show in their lifestyle. Al, in particular, really seemed to care about the other guy. People weren't viewed by him as just a means to an end. To him, profit at the plant was secondary to developing those under him — not the usual business philosophy.

At lunch Al and Chuck mostly just listened. George knew they cared, however, through their questions, responses, and apparently genuine concern for him.

Both George and Sally jumped at an invitation to join the Cranstons and a few other couples who met on Thursday nights for informal Bible study. Now for the first time they began to see what true Christianity was all about. This became apparent in the next days and weeks through the lives of these people, who were living models of what Jesus talked about.

As George was driving home one day after their first Bible study, he switched on the radio to his favorite station and listened intensely to an unexpected spot announcement — a conversation between a man and his wife. They argued. *Sounds just like Sally and me,* he thought. It was unreal! His life was being played before him! The spot closed with a calm voice simply raising the question, "Is there an answer? Is this all there is? Jesus said, 'I've come to bring meaning to life now.' Are you interested? Take that long neglected Book off the shelf and turn to the third chapter of John. You might be surprised to find that there is an answer there!"

That struck home. *What have I got to lose?* George thought.

Sally and George became regulars at that couple's group. They found love, acceptance, understanding, and the source of it all — *Christ!* Three months later both told God that they wanted to be free, that they wanted the power to live a new life. The result was *freedom* — freedom for the first time to live, to love. Purpose replaced emptiness.

CONVERSION

George and Sally had built their entire lives on one unwarranted assumption — that tensions and frustrations were the result of circumstances. Rarely, if ever, had they looked within themselves, because both, unintentionally, were really playing God. They felt they could ultimately arrive at the level of true happiness if they could just achieve and create enough of the "good things." But it had never happened. Happiness was always around the corner.

As long as they had lived with this philosophy, the Christian message was largely meaningless. "What do you mean that man is a sinner? Nonsense! Give your life to Christ? Why? That's just reaching for a crutch." Their filters were tightly closed to the gospel, and no amount of persuasion would change that!

God had begun to work in George and Sally's life, however, challenging this premise. Achievement did not bring satisfaction. There was always the nagging doubt and anxiety — an expression of the "God-shaped vacuum in the heart of every man" that Pascal talked about. They failed to recognize the source of their dissatisfaction and it continued to grow until they were grabbed by a strongly felt need for change. Gradually their perceptual filters opened and their spiritual decision processes began in earnest.

For most of their lives until that time they had probably lived somewhere between stages -5 and -4 on the model in Figure 3 (page 45). They knew something of the fundamentals of the gospel from their church background, but there certainly was not a grasp of the implications and a positive attitude. Previously they had felt no need for change because the operating premises of their life had not yet received the necessary challenge.

Sooner or later, everyone who becomes a Christian recognizes the fallacy of the "self-sufficiency assumption." This assumption lies at the heart of sin. Man does not see that the real problem resides internally. It seems to be a pervasive world view that man in his very nature is complete, having the capacity to live a full and meaningful life. Consequently, it is assumed that present problems can be remedied through education, self-effort, and material gain, along with its counterpart — revolution a la the counterculture.

This premise about man reigns supreme in contemporary education in the fields of psychology, sociology, philosophy, and education. In fact, the staunch individualism of the Western world resides on this base. Strive, achieve, get ahead, find happiness! This must stand as the supreme Satanic deception.

Inherent within the gospel message, however, is an assumption about man that is diametrically opposed to this premise. Throughout the Old and New Testaments natural man is revealed as being *incomplete*. Although created in the image of God with full rational, emotional, and volitional capacities, he cannot by his own efforts attain any real measure of goodness. He is bound to his insatiable ego-centered desires. He needs to be set free.

Acceptance of the biblical view of man leads to the meaning the gospel alone provides. That the self-centered life cannot be fulfilling is the negative message of the gospel. "He who has found his life shall lose it, and he who has lost his life for My sake shall find it" (Matt. 10:39). When this truth is accepted, the individual is at that stage of personal problem recognition (stage +3).

There are Christians who use the word "sin" as a sledge-hammer. George heard the preacher on WTLT but was turned off by him. Sin had no meaning for him as the preacher whipped him with his warnings. When he later began to grasp the full dimensions of sin and salvation, the light began to dawn.

Unfortunately, the inability of many well-meaning Christians to explain the concept of sin in meaningful terms inhibits the response to Christian witness. Al Cranston's insights at this point helped George understand his personal predicament, and the door of spiritual meaning opened.

Now, why did the callers from First Church have so little positive impact on the Calderones? Certainly their motivation was right. It is commendable that the members of First Church moved throughout the community in an attempt to share the Good News of Christ. Probably their greatest error was in failing to understand George and Sally's present spiritual status. While these two nonbelievers had many questions, there was some interest because of their growing problem recognition. They were by no means, however, ready to accept Christ at that point. It would have been better had the little "steps to God" booklet been put away and not used. Unfortunately, it appears that the church callers were trained only in its use.

The callers also erred in a depersonalized attitude that viewed George and Sally only as "candidates for the kingdom." When the latter showed no personal interest during the visit, the church visitors never returned. Undoubtedly, these visitors reported in the "sharing session" at First Church that they failed in their witness at the Calderone home. Church visitation success could be defined only in terms of the numbers who "prayed" and "decided for Christ."

How much better it would have been had the callers skill-fully evaluated the position of George and Sally in the decision process. What these people needed more than anything else was a "model" of the Christian life. The callers might have built that bridge through friendship had they been taught more effectively and had they been more perceptive. The Cranstons and the Richards did provide that model.

Radio played a significant role in George's experience. Granted, WTLT was more of a hindrance than a help, but the Christian spot on his favorite FM station grabbed him hard. The sponsors knew a great deal about the lifestyles of those listeners weaving their way home from work on the free-ways. The signal was clear, and George heard it! There was no preaching, not even an attempt at persuasion. The spon-sors knew that most potential listeners were in the earlier stages of their decision processes. Consequently, the objective was to stimulate interest and to arouse the listener to investi-gate God's Good News.

Success could be expected because some would be moved in their decision processes closer to understanding Christ. Few, however, would accept Christ immediately as a result of the spot message. The objective was to develop interest and movement in the decision process. Actual conversion usually comes through the personal witness of concerned Christians. The radio message and personal witness, therefore, work to-gether in a multimedia strategy.

Finally, when the time came for George and Sally to accept the fact and reality of Christ, they saw how His message answered their problems and met their needs. The major problem had been lack of meaning and this was reflected in many ways — in their marriage, in the rearing of their chil-dren, in George's tensions at work. In addition, they were desperately lonely people living in an impersonal world. Their limited friendships were only superficial and never even began to fill the void in their lives. Through the friendship of the Cranstons and the others in their circle, the Bible began to provide living meaning for their day-to-day existence. Christ's promise of the abundant life moved from the abstract to the concrete in their experience.

George and Sally came to Christ in *their* way. The distinctiveness of the gospel is that there is no one normative experience. Nevertheless, there are some common elements. First is acceptance of what the Bible says about man, leading to an acknowledgment and confession of personal responsibility for sin. Next is an understanding of the biblical provisions for fundamental life issues. Finally, an awareness of the practical means of relating God's provision to one's personal needs. Conversion may occur suddenly or gradually but it always comes when the individual agrees with God about his own nature and is open and receptive to Christ's claims. A new life of freedom then begins, following simple acceptance of what God says.

UNDERSTANDING DECISION PROCESSES

The gospel had been simply an abstraction to George and Sally. The statement "God loves you and has a wonderful plan for your life" is indeed a most profound truth and therefore difficult for many to comprehend. Until this truth is made personal to one's own life, to one's unique struggles and joys, it is only an abstraction. The gospel communicator has the obligation to focus theological truth in such a way that it brings light upon each person's unique situation. This, of course, cannot be done only by pontificating in the pulpit or by occupying the pew. Witnessing for Christ requires contact with people.

Unfortunately, evangelistic training in recent years appears to have neglected the decision-process perspective. Finely honed tools of persuasion, using precise language to explain gospel fundamentals, are neatly buttressed by appropriate Scripture references. Such tools are vitally necessary, but somehow the shift of focus has been away from people toward refinement of the message.

A true communicator never begins by focusing on other people as candidates for the gospel. Rather, he lives in an attitude of love, seeking to focus that love on the life of another so that the one who is the object of his love and concern can be set free. This requires sharply defined information in the following categories: (1) lifestyle and desires, (2) spiritual awareness, (3) attitudes toward the gospel, (4) decision-making styles, and (5) cultural norms and values.

Lifestyle and Desires

When Al Cranston and Chuck Richards had lunch with George, Al asked a very revealing question. He inquired, "George, what would you say is the one area of your life where you are hurting the most right now?"

George quickly replied, "I guess I would have to say that I don't see any meaning in life at all. The longer I live, the less satisfied I am, and I just wonder if anyone cares."

By this reply George revealed that he was another victim of the most pervasive problems of the modern era — loneliness and a sense of meaninglessness brought about by depersonalization.[1] This seems to be a natural accompaniment of a world of future shock in which the pace of change inhibits the ability to cope. He further indicated that those very things he once thought were so important no longer really mattered and that he was now desperately seeking real answers. Over a period of time Al and the others were able to use this knowledge under the guidance of the Holy Spirit to show George and Sally precisely how Christ could meet the needs they felt so deeply.

Everyone has certain basic desired states, which he strives to fulfill and satisfy. Some will use the term "needs";[2] others call them "wants"; and still others will make reference to "basic motive patterns." The precise terminology is completely unimportant; call these desired states what you will. What is most significant is that we understand something of what makes people tick and the implications for communication of the gospel.

One of the most helpful guides to understanding has been provided by psychologist Maslow, who has introduced the

---

[1] This is analyzed with clarity by Keith Miller in *The Becomers* (Waco, Texas: Word Books, 1973), pp. 32ff.

[2] For one of the clearest discussions see Ward Goodenough, *Cooperation in Change* (New York: Russell Sage Foundation, 1963), ch. 3.

concept of a hierarchy of needs or desired states.[3] While his writings differ somewhat on the number of such needs, usually they fall into five categories as follows:

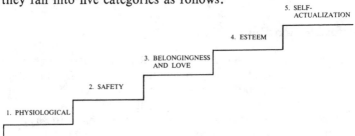

Physiological or bodily needs are foundational, and each of the others is considered to be of a different or higher order. The significance lies in the fact that no higher-order desired state will serve as a motivator until the levels below it are satisfied. The hungry man, for example, will not be very much interested in ideological discussions until he has had a good meal. Each level is full of significance in terms of understanding people.

Physiological. Into this category fall the basic bodily desires, such as hunger and thirst. If these desires are unsatisfied, all resources of the human being are focused toward satisfying them. The master communicator, Jesus Christ, was supremely aware of the hierarchy of needs. When physiological need dominated, He ministered at that point first through His healing touch. Somehow certain evangelical leaders have forgotten the example of the master communicator and have come to regard this type of social concern as being somehow secondary to communication of the gospel. But if the gospel we offer doesn't minister to the whole man, then we are using only a caricature of the message practiced and taught by Jesus. No, let's put our tracts aside when physiological need dominates and put first things first. Until we have demonstrated a proper concern at this level, we really are not serving as Christ's spokesmen.

Safety. Man also has basic concerns about security, physical

---

[3] See A. H. Maslow, *Motivation and Human Behavior,* rev. ed. (New York: Harper & Row, 1970). The implications also are developed in Miller, *The Becomers,* chs. 12 and 13.

safety, and emotional assurance. There was a time, for example, when physical hardship greatly shortened lifespans and rendered life on earth a bleak and frustrating existence. This still is the situation, of course, in some areas of the world, and it may become more widespread if food shortages and unemployment increase. Under such circumstances, it is quite proper to emphasize the great rewards of the next life. The joys of heaven and life after death can become a potent appeal of the gospel for the reason that present life has no lasting hope. The potency of this benefit wanes, however, insofar as such safety needs are met and the individual's concern has evolved to a higher order of desire.

On the other hand, future shock conditions, rapidly bring modern man back to one aspect of the safety need and that is striving to maintain the known and familiar in a chaotic world. Consequently, change is actively resisted and the familiar is maintained at all costs. Into this turmoil comes the message of the gospel with its enormous promise of freedom from anxiety and turmoil for those who take the yoke of Christ, who never changes.

Belongingness and Love. When the desires for safety and physiological satisfaction are largely met, man seems to focus on a need to give and receive love. In so doing, perhaps for the first time one perceives the role of others as of paramount significance.

It is interesting to see the extent to which this level of need has come to be dominant in the post–World War II generation in North America.[4] The parents of today's under-thirty generation were largely raised in the depression era of the 1930s, in which economic deprivation reigned supreme. Only a minority truly had these lower-order needs satisfied so that they ceased to be motivators. Not surprisingly, this generation carried a motivation for economic achievement over into the 1970s. A primary goal for them in life is economic success.

The offspring of the depression generation, however, seem to have quite a different outlook on life. Through the 1950s and

---

[4] For an explanation of the differences in motivation between generations, see James F. Engel, David T. Kollat, and Roger D. Blackwell, *Consumer Behavior*, rev. ed. (New York: Holt, Rinehart and Winston, 1973), pp. 96-108.

1960s their lower-order needs were largely met, and consequently the influence of these needs as motivators diminished. The result has been a focus on love and belonging, and if there is one area of significant current deprivation this seems to be it. The lifestyles of many parents oriented to different ends did not place the needed primacy on this area of life. As those in this generation have become young adults, this level of need still remains uppermost. In a sense, love is what is missing in George and Sally's life.

God's love and concern, when properly communicated, find receptive hearts when this area of need is keenly felt. Modern man in many quarters of the world also is yearning to know how to love others. It must be demonstrated, through our words and life, that the essence of the gospel is love and that this love takes on real meaning through healing marriages and other relationships.

Esteem. Very much related to belongingness and love is a desire for a sense of self-worth and self-respect. Nothing can be more devastating than going through life with a self-image rooted in frustration because performance misses the mark and we never can measure up. Into this void steps the living God who bases His acceptance on unconditional love and not on man's performance. "I accept you just as you are if you come to me." Nothing can be more liberating than to be released from the tyranny of perceived failure to a new self-image based on the certainty of God's love.

Self-Actualization. According to Maslow, only a small handful of people reach the stage of self-actualization, that stage in which they can give themselves to ultimate individual fulfillment through creative activities. Most have yet to find their satisfaction at the lower levels. But once this higher stage is reached, new vistas of achievement are opened. In the final analysis, however, true self-actualization is not fully possible without the indwelling power of God, without that ability simply to know and enjoy Him. The higher-order needs of knowing and understanding and aesthetics are merely subsets of self-actualization.

The Significance for the Communicator. Admittedly, the Maslow heirarchy is not perfect, and one category probably blurs into another. Yet, it provides some important clues to the basic motivations of people. Furthermore, it is probable that entire segments of a population jointly experience common needs, and this is a real aid to pinpointed communication through the mass media. For example, an appeal to college-educated young marrieds under age thirty, could logically center on the values of love and self-acceptance and strike home with a large number.

This type of information can be gathered in many ways. One way, of course, is through observation as one comes to know another. So-called "friendship evangelism" is depreciated in some quarters, but it often is the only way to discover those points of need on which the healing ministry of Christ can be focused. Another method is through questions — either asked in person or through questionnaires if the mass media are to be used. Probes are made all around another's life to find the sensitive areas, and so one may ask the following questions: "What is most important to you?" "Which of the following areas are of concern?" "How do you feel about . . . . ?"

Once again, the gospel in theological abstraction is not the gospel at all. The communicator must find those bridges into the life of another, and an analysis of desires and lifestyles is the logical starting point. The task is to show precisely how these desires may be met through the person of Christ. Goodenough has sounded a warning of supreme importance when he stated that people will not change until they *want to change,* until that change is seen as beneficial in terms of their basic needs and desires.[5]

Spiritual Awareness

A properly understood decision for Christ does not require a leap into the unknown. In fact, the experience of many evangelists is that a large number of those who appear to have committed their lives to Christ fail to show signs of regeneration. The cause often is that there was no real grasp of the implications of the gospel.

How much must a person know before a rational decision

---

[5] Goodenough, *Cooperation in Change,* ch. 3.

can be made? This is a very difficult question to answer, first of all, because there are many things that can be understood spiritually only after a life commitment is made. As Paul indicated in the second chapter of his first letter to the Corinthians, spiritual truths can be discerned only by spiritual people. Undoubtedly, reference is made here to the deeper truths necessary for growth in the Christian life; otherwise no one could ever become a Christian.

Furthermore, people differ substantially in the amount of information required before they make a major decision of any kind.[6] Some will act with only a skeleton basis of fact, whereas others will delay until they can obtain a greater measure of certainty. Full certainty, however, will never be possible; there must come a point at which a step of faith is taken.

Even while recognizing these considerations, most would agree that there is a minimum level of understanding required with respect to God, the nature of man, the uniqueness of Jesus, and the practical steps required for a life commitment to Christ.

First there must be at least an initial grasp that there is one God whose revelation of Himself through the Word of God (the Bible) declares His attributes and His reality as a personal God. Then, as has been elaborated earlier, the Bible also reveals the nature of man. It is crucial for the inquirer to understand this basic biblical premise about the nature of man: that all are incomplete and separated from God. The impact of this truth no doubt becomes much more apparent after regeneration. But the candidate for saving faith must at least be open to testing this premise. Finally, Christ's basic claims about Himself and His deity must be understood. At the very minimum, the inquirer must recognize that Christ claimed to be unique — that He is the visible expression of the unseen God and the *only* way to attain a full and meaningful life both now and in eternity. Once the individual gets to this point and is in a stage of problem recognition (having an awareness of alienation from God and feeling strongly a need

---

[6] For a review of relevant literature from a secular perspective, see Engel, Kollat, and Blackwell, *Consumer Behavior,* chs. 16-18.

for change), the last communication task is to indicate the steps necessary to come into saving belief — repentance and commitment.

If awareness is deficient in any of the above respects, it is the job of the communicator to use the proper combination of message and media to build the minimum awareness level. Furthermore, the extent to which this important task has been successfully accomplished is *measurable,* as the next chapter will demonstrate.

Attitudes Toward the Gospel

If the communicator has succeeded in speaking to felt need and building a minimum level of awareness, there should be a positive shift in attitudes toward the gospel message itself and toward its most visible manifestation — the church. The gospel, in other words, is presented as the means necessary to satisfy that basic need. If the person is progressing in his or her decision process, there will be growing interest in this alternative. For attitude shift to take place, however, it will often be necessary to counter a previously negative view toward the church.

George and Sally Calderone were not positive toward either Christianity or the church. In part, this reflected earlier negative experiences, but it also reflected ignorance of the true significance of both. Through the combined efforts of concerned lay people, radio, and books, this attitude shifted substantially. The Holy Spirit worked through it all to bring about problem recognition and to set the stage for the life-changing decision that was to come later. The combination of skillful use of message and media, then, was reflected in a pronounced favorable shift in attitude.

From this discussion it may easily be concluded that attitude change can be a useful goal for Christian communication. As will be pointed out later, this type of communication objective is pertinent in terms of signifying the desired response in the decision processes of those in the audience, *and* it is measurable.

Decision-Making Styles

There are substantial differences between groups of people in the manner in which decisions are made. In some cultures, no one will take a step of the magnitude of accepting Christ unless everyone else in the social group takes a similar step. There are numerous examples in the anthropological literature of people movements,[7] and it is common for whole tribes to become Christians at once! Under such circumstances it would be dangerous to press one individual to decide by himself and thereby risk becoming a social deviate. At one time this practice was common in mission circles, and the wreckages of family units that were unnecessarily destroyed still remain. In the final analysis, the strictly individual decision must be made, but it is a distinctly North American phenomenon to see it happen so frequently without deep soul searching as to the consequences within a family or tribal unit. The appropriate decision style, then, is often reflected in the very fabric of the culture itself, and this must not be disregarded.

Cultural Norms and Values

There are widespread differences between segments within a single culture and certainly between different cultures. Often the extent of these variations is not grasped, and the effects created when the communicator steps out of his own milieu are all too often devastating.

A group of Japanese pastors and church leaders pointed out a number of factors that make communication in the Japanese environment a far cry from its North American counterpart. Here are some of the differences elaborated on by those attending a pastoral seminar in Tokyo:

1. Social traditions require obedience to orders given by those who are perceived to be socially superior. It is unnatural to respond to a simple gospel presentation given by a social peer.
2. Religions are expected to be ritualistic and formalistic.

---

[7] See Goodenough, *Cooperation in Change,* ch. 11.

If the church does not require some type of ceremony upon joining, it will be suspect.
3. The prevalence of ancestor worship makes it difficult to believe in Christ, and Christians are accused of having no love and concern for ancestors. This has been successfully countered by greater stress on the Christian funeral and the meaning of death and of life after death.
4. Those who are fanatical for a religious cause are suspect. Too much overt enthusiasm, therefore, can be a hindrance.
5. The essence of religion is felt to be incomprehensible. Therefore, short testimonies are usually ineffective and lengthier explanations are expected.
6. Polytheism is pervasive. The idea of one God is quite unnatural and difficult to grasp.

This, of course, is just a partial listing, but the dilemmas presented are formidable. There can be no compromise in the fundamentals of the gospel message, but the way in which the message is presented *must* be adapted to these cultural norms. Greater ritualistic formality, for example, can be utilized. The short testimony and brief presentation can be modified. The great error enters when the communicator assumes that all people are the same. This, of course, is the sin of enthnocentrism discussed earlier. The overly enthusiastic American, for example, may never get to first base in talking with most Japanese, and the reverse will probably also be true. The key is to become bicultural — to develop an ability to detect sensitive cultural differences and to modify behavior accordingly. This is necessary when the white suburbanite goes into the black ghetto or into the deep rural south or to another country of the world.

IS THERE ANY HOPE, THEN, FOR THE AVERAGE PERSON?

Probably by now the reader is about to assume that there is no hope for him to be an effective communicator out in that world. It might look as if each of us will have to carry a mini-computer just to store all those things we must know, but this is not true at all.

It is surprising how much can be discovered in just a five- or ten-minute conversation. Those points of felt need, spiritual awareness, attitudes, cultural backgrounds, etc, may soon become quite apparent to the discerning observer. The key is to put your "spiritual antenna" up so that you will be able to understand people. This ability to diagnose spiritual status and to place the person accurately on the continuum in Figure 3, may be learned and developed by any Christian.

We do feel, however, that much of the training in evangelistic communication now offered to the layman is naive and simplistic. The real need is to teach people first to diagnose spiritual status and then to develop facility in using the Word of God to speak precisely and accurately to the need that people feel in terms they can comprehend. The simple tracts now used are largely successful only when the other person already has considerable Christian background, is at a stage of problem recognition (stage -3), and simply needs a practical stimulus to accept Christ. As useful as these tools are, they are only a start in developing a communication ability that can be adapted to any situation that might arise.

6

Men, the Message, and the Media

The Calderones are just two of the more than 40,000 people who live in Rollingwood. Probably no more than 20 percent of these 40,000 are Christians, judging at least by church-attendance figures. So the tasks of proclamation and persuasion are far from finished.

What must be done to reach the community? This question looms large in the deliberations of First Church and, in one way or another, in most of the other churches in the area. One church, for example, is about to carry out a door-to-door Bible distribution plan in cooperation with a Bible society. Another is planning to present a series of evangelistic messages by its pastor over radio station WTLT. Still others are considering neighborhood calling and canvassing. The only problem is that seldom, if ever, have these churches considered a cooperative strategy that could make a demonstrable difference on the community. Each seems to be aiming its own little garden hose at a forest fire. Tom Bartlett learned to his sorrow at the second meeting he attended of the Rollingwood Ministerial Fellowship that interchurch cooperation stops pretty much at the point of pious statements and an occasional community service offered at Christmas or Easter.

To one degree or another Rollingwood is a good example of the picture throughout the world. Consider, for example, the situation in Japan. Only about 1 percent of 107 million people profess to be Christians, and, although the church is growing, it is not keeping up with the increase in the population.[1] In Japan there are 43 denominations that have more than 1,000 members; 140 Protestant mission agencies with

---

[1] These figures are taken from the "Status of Christianity, Coun-

2,400 individual missionaries; several major interdenominational broadcasting agencies; and a Christian literature ministry consisting of 90 publishers, 25 major presses, and over 70 bookstores. Yet, seldom has there been any real attempt to develop a unified strategy utilizing the strengths of the various groups in such a way that their individual distinctiveness is maintained while they make a genuine contribution to a virile, cooperative outreach. The need for such an outreach is increasingly being recognized, however, and a number of significant steps are now underway.

Let's face it: *the Great Commission cannot and will not be fulfilled unless the individualistic and even separatistic tendencies of evangelical Christians are lowered with the objective of mounting a multiple-church, multiple-media strategy.* Do not read this statement as a plea for the ecumenical movement — rather, it is a plea for *unity without union,* without compromise of what each fellowship perceives the biblical imperatives to be.

Some may object to the above statement, but is there any other alternative? Can we escape the fact that after two thousand years the harvest is yet to be gathered? Hardly! It is time to combine our resources, which at best are all too limited, and concentrate our firepower so that it can make a real impact.

A multiple-church, multiple-media campaign must not be based on program orientation, or the mistakes of the past will only be repeated. Furthermore, a properly conceived adaptive strategy will require a formalized process of planning enriched and guided by the Holy Spirit (Prov. 16:9). There are always three foundations for an adaptive strategy: (1) experience — especially when rigorous attempts are made to learn from past successes and failures; (2) intuition — that "sixth sense" that enables some decision-makers to decipher facts and arrive at the core of the issue; and (3) research. Research is usually the one base that is neglected, but this oversight can be fatal in a world of rapid change. Indeed, all three bases are required if we are to comprehend the tasks before us.

What are the steps in a research-based, multiple-church,

---

try Profile" on Japan prepared for the International Congress on World Evangelization held in Lausanne in July, 1974.

multiple-media strategy? These should be familiar to the reader by now:

1. analysis of the environment
2. assessment of organizational strengths and weaknesses
3. determination of measurable goals
4. determination of the strategy (message and media)
5. execution of the strategy
6. measurement of effectiveness
7. evaluation (post mortem)

Many of these concepts have been discussed in the preceding pages, but there will be an obvious difference between the analytical rigor required to lead one person to Christ and that required for an entire segment of hundreds or even thousands.

ANALYSIS OF THE ENVIRONMENT

Obviously, any strategy begins with an understanding of the audience, but attention also must be focused on several additional factors: (1) competition, (2) governmental regulations, and (3) media resources.

The Audience

George and Sally Calderone represent a segment of the total audience in Rollingwood, albeit a very small one. Obviously, a strategy that moves beyond face-to-face communication must contend with much larger segments. A major goal of the environmental analysis is to uncover segments of people who are essentially alike in terms of lifestyles and backgrounds and who show evidence of receptivity and openness to change.

When one thinks about it, the mass media will tend to be ineffective if those in the audience are greatly different from one another in any important respect. After all, only one message can be used at a time, and it can easily wind up missing the mark with most people under these circumstances. Therefore, strategy begins with the isolation of *homogeneous* segments, most often defined in such measurable terms as age, educational background, or lifestyle.[2] In that way there is a

_____

[2] For a discussion of the procedures used in audience segmentation, see James F. Engel, Hugh G. Wales, and Martin R. Warshaw,

much greater probability that an appropriate combination of message and media will succeed in influencing many rather than a few.

Experience and intuition will be of help in defining these segments, but it usually is necessary also to utilize some form of research. Let it be stated at the outset that research is nothing more than the gathering of information useful for purposes of planning and decision making. It is never an end in itself. This may seem to be an obvious point, but experience has shown that it is easy to get sidetracked on the exotic issues of research and forget the fact that the real focus must *always* remain on planning. In the final analysis, such information provides the objective basis upon which the Holy Spirit can then build as He guides us through the renewing of our minds (Rom. 12:2).

Careful personal observation and skillful questioning will be an adequate approach to research in face-to-face communication or when groups are small and people are well-known to each other. Larger segments, however, will usually require utilization of some type of survey instrument. The purpose of this book is not to delve deeply into research technique. Let it be noted that there is a well-developed methodology that utilizes questionnaires to study relatively small samples out of a larger group.[3] Furthermore, experience has shown that this methodology may be adapted so that it is useful almost anywhere in the world.[4] Surely, God's people also should make use of any tool that can be helpful in carrying out His work.

Two areas, in particular, require a careful analysis of the audience: (1) determination of audience target and (2) assessment of the requirements of the message.

Audience Target. From the discussion thus far, it is appar-

Promotional Strategy, 3rd ed. (Homewood, Ill.: Richard D. Irwin, Inc., 1975), ch. 9.

[3] An especially useful manual for this purpose is C. H. Backstrom and G. D. Hursh, *Survey Research* (Evanston, Illinois: Northwestern University Press, 1963).

[4] An excellent unpublished manual has been prepared by Wilbur Schramm of Stanford University documenting the fact that surveys now are used for a wide variety of purposes in nearly every corner of the world.

ent that there are differences among various segments in the
degree to which they will be responsive to the gospel message.
Felt need for change, of course, is the most basic sign of this
openness, and its existence is a positive indication that the
Holy Spirit is at work bringing about conviction and problem
recognition.

Openness to change comes about as people begin to re-
appraise their self-image, usually as a result of the impact of
some kind of new experience.[5] The Muslim college-age student
in Indonesia, for example, was virtually impenetrable with the
gospel until the post-Sukarno era when his country emerged
into dynamic economic development and growth. New experiential vistas opened, educational opportunity burgeoned, and
previous religious values began to be challenged. For the first
time, many grasped altogether new opportunities for individual
achievement. Therefore, those who are now in college are
particularly interested in, and responsive to, the gospel. In
short, their filters have been broken wide open by new experience, and this is an ideal time to focus efforts both to proclaim
the gospel and to persuade.

Another factor to look for is the strength of existing religious and/or philosophical belief. A fundamental principle
of persuasion is that attitude change proceeds in proportion
to the strength of presently held attitudes. Therefore, the
nominal people of all faiths *can* (but not necessarily *will*)
represent a responsive audience segment.[6] The converse of
this generalization also is true in that efforts generally are
wasted when they are directed to those who hold their convictions deeply. This was recognized by the Lord who achieved
little response among the Pharisees and concentrated instead
on the publicans and sinners who keenly felt their need for
change and recognized the inadequacy of their existing beliefs.

Which segments are likely to be most responsive to the
gospel in Rollingwood? Keep in mind that Rollingwood in
marketing terms is considered to be "upscale"; i.e., it represents those in the higher educational, occupational, and social

---

[5] Ward Goodenough, *Cooperation in Change* (New York: Russell
Sage Foundation, 1963), p. 219.

[6] See Donald A. McGavran, *How Churches Grow* (New York:
Friendship Press, 1955), p. 50.

strata. There are relatively few who would be viewed as blue-collar or working-class people. The majority work in the city and are commuters.

The key to success is to identify groups where most, for one reason or another, are faced with circumstances of change and with the necessity of "reprogramming" their perceptual filters. Obviously, those of high school or college age qualify, and it is probable, at least given the current experience elsewhere throughout most of the world, that they would represent a responsive segment. But what about those commuters? Are the strivings of materialism wearing thin as was the case with George Calderone? Are circumstances such that there is a recognized need for change?

Quite likely, the young business executive living in Rollingwood is no different from the majority of three thousand business executives who were studied by the American Management Association and who voiced deep concern about imposed pressures to compromise personal standards to meet company goals.[7] It is small wonder that 85 percent of all managers undergo a deep personal conflict when they discover their youthful ideals and goals run counter to business operations that seem to be low on principle and high on expediency.[8] This conflict is most severe between the ages of thirty-four and forty-two, and it is often manifested by unwillingness to take on new problems and a desire to minimize the total demands of a job on one's life. Some will accept the advice of one executive who noted the contradictions he faced but concluded that it is necessary to "play by the rules of the game" if one is to accumulate much money or power.[9] But others will not willingly take this route and are searching instead for the personal power that will enable them to "dare to be different."

Many of these same executives are experiencing equally severe tensions at home. Divorce rates soar among those in this segment. Others continue the scramble to raise their

---

[7] Cited in *Business Week* (September 15, 1973), p. 178.

[8] Cited in *Sales Management* (May 1, 1969), p. 20.

[9] See A. C. Carr, "Is Business Loving Ethical?" in J. R. Wish and S. H. Gamble, eds., *Marketing and Social Issues* (New York: John Wiley & Sons, Inc., 1971), p. 107.

standard of living, only to find that this desire is insatiable.

This segment of business executives (and their wives) under the age of forty from every perspective seems potentially to be open and responsive to the gospel message. The remainder of our discussion will focus on this audience target, for purposes of illustration, although there are other equally responsive segments, especially the youth.

Message Requirements. Definition of audience target is only the first step, of course. Next, it is necessary to focus the research inquiry on the following questions: (1) lifestyle and desires, (2) spiritual awareness, (3) attitudes toward the gospel, (4) decision-making styles, and (5) norms and values. The importance of each of these items of information was discussed in the preceding chapter, and one category obviously blurs into another. The main point here is that some type of questionnaire survey will be required to isolate this information, without which it will be impossible to mount an effective adaptive strategy.

Let it be assumed that such a study was undertaken in Rollingwood by a committee appointed by the local churches and that the data in Figure 4 were the outcome.

What implications emerge as you study Figure 4? Notice first of all that we must work with averages. There never is complete unanimity of response, so it is necessary to focus on the answers given by the majority. Second, there are definite signs that this segment contains a number who are open to change. Materialistic striving is the dominant lifestyle as is to be expected, but its motivational impact is diminishing and real questions are being raised by many about the very goals of life. Also, the mid-career conflict discussed above is very much in evidence. The spiritual awareness indicates that most have reached only the stage of initial awareness and interest as depicted in Figure 3 (perhaps stage -5). There is substantial confusion and misinformation, and these must be cleared up if many are to accept Christ soon. The result, of course, is that attitudes toward the gospel and the Church are mixed.

These data are of significance in communication strategy. They demonstrate openness to change and make apparent the sources of existing areas of felt need. Furthermore, a precise

Lifestyle

The majority agreed with the following statements:

> To me it is important to have the latest things in my home.
>
> I place great satisfaction in a steady advance toward the top in my career.
>
> I very much enjoy world travel.
>
> I want my children to have the best in a college education.
>
> I enjoy facing a difficult challenge on the job.
>
> Those who know me well would see me as one who wants to get ahead in the world.

But openness to change was indicated by substantial agreement with statements such as these:

> There are times when I feel I must compromise my personal convictions at work.
>
> Sometimes I wonder if getting ahead on the job is worth it.
>
> I have a growing concern that my marriage isn't what it once was.
>
> Often now I find myself less satisfied with the general direction of my life.
>
> Frequently I consider the possibility of doing something altogether different with my life.

Spiritual Status

> 68 percent believe there is one God.
>
> 48 percent believe that most of the problems in the world today are a result of man himself.
>
> 68 percent believe that Jesus actually lived on this earth.
>
> 40 percent feel confident that Jesus experienced a bodily resurrection.
>
> 41 percent indicated agreement that Jesus has provided the way to know God personally.
>
> 54 percent have read the Bible at least once in the past year.
>
> 29 percent could correctly state how one becomes a Christian.

Attitudes Toward the Gospel and Church

> 47 percent attended church at least once in the past year.
>
> 59 percent evidence doubt that the church actually has personal significance for them.
>
> 67 percent were interested in knowing more about Christianity.

Figure 4. The Results of a Survey of Suburban Men Under Age Forty Undertaken by Rollingwood Churches

indication of present spiritual awareness and attitude is given. It becomes obvious that the messages must demonstrate how a personal relationship with Jesus Christ can provide real meaning at home and on the job. They must clearly show that Christ is the only plausible solution to these problems.

Competition

By competition is meant those other viewpoints that are competing for men's minds. In many parts of the world, potent competition is provided by non-Christian religions, and this is increasingly true in the United States. Under such circumstances, at least part of the strategy must counter these competing claims. In Rollingwood the competing philosophy is materialism, the significance of which has already been reviewed.

Governmental Regulations

It is obvious that laws and regulations define the "playing field" for communication strategy. Unfortunately, the obvious is not always given the consideration it deserves. For example, the Federal Communications Commission in the United States enforces a rule referred to as the "fairness doctrine." In brief, this rule stipulates that any partisan viewpoint expressed over the air, especially in the political arena, must carry with it the opportunity for opposing points of view to be expressed also. As of this writing, the fairness doctrine has not yet been interpreted to apply to the Christian message, although there is growing sentiment that the airing of the Christian position should be followed by equal opportunity for others. This, of course, would substantially change the complexion of gospel broadcasting. There is no question, however, that open attacks on individuals or groups over the air must allow for rebuttal under the fairness doctrine. One well-known religious broadcaster is at the time of this writing engaged in substantial litigation over this very issue, and the outcome is unclear.

Another regulation of real significance in the mass media

pertains to truth in advertising. Any paid message run in media that cover more than one state falls under the purview of the Federal Trade Commission, which has the obligation of monitoring the veracity of claims. As yet, Christian communicators appear to have escaped scrutiny, but what would happen if the searchlight is turned their way? Would examples of deception and false and misleading claims be unearthed? One radio station analyzed by Wheaton graduate students solicits support from churches, making the claim that five million are being reached for Christ, whereas all available evidence indicates that no more than 2 percent of that number, or 100,000, are actually being reached. There is no way to avoid the fact that this claim is an exaggeration. Perhaps it is made in ignorance, but that is hardly an excuse. The absolute truth is increasingly demanded of the secular communicator in these days of consumerism, and why should Christians be exempt?

Media Resources

Finally, the environmental analysis also should center on the availability of mass-media resources. Rollingwood has three radio stations — WTLT and two secular stations. In addition, it is reached by twenty-four other radio stations and five television stations whose programs are beamed from the adjacent city and surrounding suburbs. There is one daily evening paper and two papers published weekly for various neighborhoods, plus the papers that come from the city. The local media, in particular, can be used in one way or another, especially for purposes of proclamation if it seems appropriate for other reasons to do so.

Implications

The environmental analysis has disclosed one segment, among others, that seems to be particularly "ripe for harvest." The major source of competition for the minds and hearts of people is materialism, but there is growing doubt about its efficacy. Media resources exist for the communication task, and there are no particular governmental restrictions other than those that apply to all communicators. Therefore, a golden opportunity exists.

ASSESSMENT OF ORGANIZATIONAL STRENGTHS AND WEAKNESSES

The next question centers on the availability of resources needed to capitalize on the opportunity that has been demonstrated. This is especially critical if only one organization, say a local church (or a mission board in an overseas situation), must design and execute the strategy.

One church, for example, conducted a community analysis that, although not as extensive as the one described here, disclosed a similar situation with two possible audience segments. A review by the elders led to the conclusion, however, that the strengths of the individual members, plus some limitations on other resources within the church, made a focus on high school and college students most feasible. In short, there was no attempt to be *all things to all people*. It was recognized that, after all, there are other churches in the area and that the total task can be accomplished only cooperatively. Under the guidance of the Holy Spirit, this church worked in its area of strength.

Undoubtedly, the combined resources of the cooperating churches in Rollingwood could meet the challenge. Furthermore, there is opportunity to draw upon various interdenominational organizations that can provide real assistance in such areas as evangelistic training, design and placement of radio spot announcements, etc.

DETERMINATION OF MEASURABLE GOALS

We have now arrived at a crucial stage — the establishment of goals. The usual tendency is to state the goal something like this: "to saturate Rollingwood with the claims of Christ during 1976." But this is only a general statement of purpose and it is little more than a platitude, at that. How could one ever know if the job is accomplished? A goal must be measurable or it is of no functional value.

Careful use must now be made of the audience analysis. The awareness and attitude data provide some valuable benchmarks. In other words, an indication is given of current levels of spiritual awareness and attitude, and the purpose of the campaign must be to improve these levels. Notice that the task now is primarily one of proclamation rather than persuasion because of low awareness of gospel fundamentals. Most of those in this segment will not respond, at least initially, to a simple presentation that presses for a decision. Decisions for Christ, of course, are always the ultimate goal, but there is a real need here to bring people to that point in the model of spiritual decision processes (Figure 3, page 45) where they both understand the implications of the gospel and have a positive attitude toward it (and the Church). If this can be done, the stage is set for largescale later response to persuasion (i.e., a call for decision).

It is at this point that the planners must focus on prayer to be sure that they have the very mind of Christ. In other words, what does the Head of the Church want to accomplish through the Holy Spirit? To some extent, accomplishments will be limited by available resources. To a degree, at least, the more we have to spend, the more we can expect to happen. But such considerations cannot be the final determinant of the goals that are set. Rather, an assurance of the Spirit's leading the church to take certain necessary action must be the outcome of prayer.

The difficulty in goal-determination is to specify the amount of change it is reasonable to expect. This problem is faced by the secular communicator as well, of course,[10] and there really is no substitute for experience. The expectations at the outset may be unrealistic, but one must start with something. Goals, after all, are not figures to be etched in stone. It is to be expected that modifications will be introduced over a period of time.

What form should these goals take? There must be a statement of the expected changes in benchmark figures as a

---

[10] See Engel, Wales, and Warshaw, *Promotional Strategy*, ch. 9.

result of the campaign. For example, it might be decided to increase the percentage of those —

1. who believe there is one God from 68% to 75%.
2. who believe that most of the problems in the world today are a result of man himself (i.e., man is a sinner) from 48% to 75%.
3. who feel confident that Jesus experienced a bodily resurrection from 40% to 70%.
4. who agree that Jesus provides the way to know God personally from 41% to 70%.
5. who have read the Bible at least once in the past year from 54% to 75%.
6. who can correctly state how one becomes a Christian from 29% to 70%.
7. who have attended church at least once in the past year from 47% to 70%.

In addition, a goal for attitude change could be to reduce the doubt that Christianity has personal significance from 59% to 35%.

It is also reasonable to expect a certain number of decisions for Jesus Christ. An actual numerical objective to this end should be set, and each cooperating church should specify the number for which it assumes responsibility. This should be realized in demonstrable growth in the membership of each church, and goals should be set for this factor as well.

Again, these goals are only illustrative, but it is obvious that reaching them would signify a substantial cooperative attainment. One year later it might also be found that certain of the goals were overly optimistic, but that does not necessarily indicate failure. The great benefit is that all the churches in the Christian community have been aiming toward the same target, and this cannot help but represent a giant step forward.

DESIGN AND EXECUTION OF THE STRATEGY

The precision with which the goals were set will prove to be of great assistance in the determination of the communication strategy. While one cannot, in the final analysis, separate the decisions necessary for message and for media, there are some considerations that are unique to each.

Message

The gospel, of course, is not relevant if it is communicated as an abstraction. This requires that the messages utilized in the various media speak directly to the needs of people in areas such as marriage, occupation, and materialism. The lifestyle data cited only in summary form in Figure 4 are invaluable for this purpose. In this context, then, it is necessary also to focus on showing that man is a sinner and that Jesus provides the key to satisfaction of felt need. In particular, it will be required to center on raising awareness about the resurrection and the very uniqueness of Jesus. In addition, the Bible and the Church must be stressed as part of the solution.

The final execution will be the outcome of creative thinking guided and enriched by the Holy Spirit. Creativity is, after all, not pure imagination — rather, it is *disciplined* imagination, with the discipline provided by the goals and by the leadership of the Spirit. Unfortunately, or perhaps fortunately, there are no rules to be followed in moving from goal to message, a fact long since discovered by the advertiser.[11] While there is a broad sense in which creative writing and communication are guided by rules of syntax and logic, the latitude for individual creativity looms large.

Audience lifestyle imposes yet another form of discipline on creative imagination. Certain patterns of wording, phrasing, and emphasis obviously will be more acceptable than others. Stained-glass words such as "saved," "washed in the blood," "justification," and others all have legitimate theological meaning, but their connotation to the outside world is pure jargon. Linguists long ago learned to find the "functional equivalent" for such words when translated into the everyday language of the people. Functional equivalents also must be found when communicating with those in any given segment. Remember George Calderone's reaction when he heard a preacher scream the word "sinner" at him on WTLT? It is

---

[11] See Ibid., ch. 13.

literally true that George is a sinner, but the strategy used to reach him was badly off the mark at that point.

Once again, we must also contend with that ever-present danger — ethnocentrism. While it may be less of a problem when one is communicating with the Rollingwood suburbanite than it would be, say, in Nigeria, the danger is always present. It is encountered most frequently beyond North American borders by assuming that everyone follows Western rules of logic: A plus B; therefore C. This is a type of linear thought pattern engrained in our makeup, but it is often totally absent elsewhere. It is not unusual for an oriental to embrace simultaneously certain thought patterns that, to us, appear to be completely inconsistent. It may not work to point out logical inconsistencies or to expose the fallacies of basic presuppositions. An entirely different tack must then be taken in message strategy.

Ethnocentrism has been compounded by the all-too-frequent practice of translating Western books, tracts, articles, and broadcast programs in non-Western settings. The vast majority of the mass-media content used overseas has, especially in past years, been written elsewhere. It is only by accident that such a transplanted style and thought pattern can strike home in a radically different context. Such a practice is of debatable merit, and where it still prevails its perpetuation should cease as soon as possible. The only reasonable alternative is to train and develop national writers.

Just one last point should be stressed here. American evangelicals are prone to criticize any type of evangelistic communication that does not present the plan of salvation. Many would, for example, insist that everything said to the Rollingwood suburbanite should press for that decision. But consider the probable response! The communication will probably be ignored or even reacted to negatively, unless the recipient has reached the stage of problem recognition (stage -3) and is thus open to persuasion as defined in Figure 3. The goal of proclamation, on the other hand, is *to move people toward decision, not to call for decision!* It is particularly tragic that the well-meaning layman who must often pay the bills for his type of outreach also feels this gives him the authority to straightjacket the strategy in inappropriate ways.

Remember, if the stated goals have been accomplished, this represents successful evangelism, even if there are *not* great numbers of decisions *at the present time*.

Media

The most fundamental consideration in selecting the communication media is to *go where the prospects are!* This implies, in a North American setting at least, that it is becoming increasingly unreasonable to expect many to gather at church for an evangelistic service. People exercise a unique ability to avoid exposure when they know they are a target for persuasive communication, and this is particularly true in an environment where the Church is suspect. Let it also be clearly noted, however, that this is by no means true worldwide. In fact, quite the opposite is often the case in South America, for example. Thus it is impossible to present hard and fast generalizations about media. All that can be stated are some general factors that tend to hold true in most situations.

Secular Radio. Radio is one of the most remarkable media of our time. In even the most underdeveloped countries of the world, most people are within the reach of a radio set. Listenership in the more advanced areas is phenomenal. In the United States, for example, the average household has more than five radio sets,[12] and over 90 percent of all adults in Australia listen to commercial radio on a given day.[13] It is a highly personal medium that can be enjoyed in almost any setting.

Radio has long been used as a significant means of proclaiming the gospel. Missionary shortwave radio spans the globe continuously and plays a valuable role in stimulating awareness of, and interest in, the gospel. Missionary radio in Haiti has done such an effective job in proclamation that door-to-door witness by laymen now invariably sees unprecedented numbers of true and lasting decisions for Jesus Christ. The role of radio in "effecting" actual conversions, however, is

---

[12] "Radio Reach Is Everywhere — Homes, Autos, Outdoors," *Advertising Age* (November 21, 1973), p. 100.

[13] Alan Nichols, *The Communicators* (Sydney: Pilgrim Productions, Ltd., 1972), p. 63.

much less, although it can and does happen. As a general rule, radio is best used for proclamation.

George Calderone was significantly affected by a spot announcement on his way home. That announcement struck him right at his point of need. Furthermore, it did not turn him off by "churchy" words. Rather, it accomplished much by stimulating his interest in the fact that the gospel might have something real to say about his current dilemma. He was reached *where he was* in terms that were most meaningful to him.

The Rollingwood strategy could make legitimate use of similar spot announcements. If these are placed to be aired during driving times to and from work, there could be some real gains in both awareness and attitude shift.

Christian Radio. Some churches would quickly turn to a Christian radio station and solicit its help in this outreach. Generally, however, this would be most inappropriate. This probably is a controversial conclusion, and the reasons need to be stated clearly. Remember the human tendency to avoid unwanted communication. This is referred to as selective exposure. The result is that Christian radio stations (i.e., those airing mostly programs of hymns and preaching) reach Christians almost exclusively. There are some exceptions, of course, and an occasional person is converted, but these are the *exceptions and not the rule.* The major role of Christian radio is to cultivate the Christian.

Television. Much that was said about secular radio may also be said about television. It, too, is becoming a worldwide medium, and only those who are most isolated or most impoverished are beyond its reach. In the United States it is watched over six hours a day by the average person,[14] and viewing time in Australia exceeds three hours.[15] Furthermore, people genuinely like television and turn to it as their favorite medium for entertainment and escape.[16]

Presently, Rollingwood is reached only by stations from the larger city. Thus, it would be inadvisable to consider any use

---

[14] A. C. Nielsen figures, February, 1973.

[15] Nichols, *The Communicators*, p. 14.

[16] See Robert T. Bower, *Television and the Public* (New York: Holt, Rinehart and Winston, Inc., 1973).

of television, because of wasted coverage. But what will happen as cable television and community antenna systems grow? About 25 percent of American homes will soon be wired for cable television,[17] and this could quickly make dozens of channels available for use right in Rollingwood. The church now has a great opportunity if this new advancement is used correctly.

The very *worst* strategy (let us repeat, the very worst strategy) would be to purchase television equipment (which is becoming quite inexpensive) and rush on the air with something such as a church service. Unfortunately, this very suggestion was recently made in a widely disseminated trade publication, although other writers were much more cautious.[18] Always keep the viewers' psychology uppermost in mind. Experience to date indicates the only ones who are most likely to watch a televised church service are those members who decided to stay home that morning. If a person won't go to a worship service in a church building, why will he watch it on the screen? What we don't need now is a rush to this medium with ill-conceived, "home-made," poorly-thought-out strategies.

In the future it might be appropriate to explore production of locally originated shows for local cable TV, focusing on real people and presenting their Christian experience in a realistic and credible fashion. Other shows might feature the work of the church in meeting community needs and in other areas of service.

Print. Books, tracts, and magazines will always be useful tools for persuasion and proclamation (assuming people can read). The advantage is that the content may be pinpointed to the individual in terms of his current state of need, spiritual status, and lifestyle. Such magazines as *Faith at Work, Campus Life, Guideposts, and Collegiate Challenge* have been especially effective for this purpose when distributed by discerning lay people. In addition, certain Christian books have sold remarkably well in the secular market worldwide, the most notable

---

[17] Engel, Wales, and Warshaw, *Promotional Strategy,* ch. 11.
[18] See the various articles on cable television in *Religious Broadcasting* (April-May, 1974).

recent example being *The Late Great Planet Earth*.[19] That book speaks effectively to concerns on the minds of the masses, and the gospel is presented with great clarity in this context. Books of this kind are often distributed in secular outlets such as drugstores and supermarkets, and sales are often quite high. Similar experience with other Christian books is also reported from other literate countries like Japan.

Films. In many parts of the world film is one of the best evangelistic tools. The key, of course, is to present content that is of interest over and beyond its Christian message. Often whole communities will gather for such an occasion. This may also be true in a North American country, the success of Billy Graham films and the Moody Science films being two cases in point. Once again, the greatest impact usually is in proclamation — building awareness and interest — although the yield of decisions also may be high at times.

Audio cassettes. The audio cassette is a recent medium gaining popularity since the onset of inexpensive tape playback units. There has been some careful experimentation, especially in Thailand and other Asian countries, in the use of this medium as an evangelistic tool. It seems to be most appropriately used after the stage of initial awareness and interest has been reached. In this way, tapes may be carefully chosen and tailored to the individual. There are numerous instances in which tapes have been used to bring people right to the point of decision. Surprisingly, the tape has even surpassed personal witness in bringing Muslims in Asia to make an initial decision for Christ.

In nonliterate countries, the audio cassette represents an underutilized medium. In Indonesia, for example, six major Christian publishers are producing books for a population in which 90 percent or more have neither sufficient literacy nor the economic means to permit the purchase of a book. In such instances, this is a gross waste of the resources of the church. How much better if the same resources were placed into the mass distribution of tape players and tapes. This strategy has been used in Thailand, and missionaries often find whole tribes or communities predisposed and ready to

[19] Hal Lindsey, *The Late Great Planet Earth* (Grand Rapids: Zondervan Publishing House, 1970).

accept Christ when they are afterward given the opportunity to do so through personal witness.

Cassettes could be utilized in Rollingwood, although their distribution must be through laymen. George Calderone, for example, might have been given cassettes and he could have been helped in this manner to see the meaning of the Christian answer to his problems.

Lay witness. There is no question that lay witness *generally* will be the most effective way to bring people to decision. It possesses high credibility and it obviously is the most personal of all media. *Rarely will a segment be effectively evangelized through the mass media without personal witness.*

We saw an example of how concerned laymen reached the Calderones by personal witness. They did so on the basis of a keen understanding of their backgrounds and spiritual status. In this sense, they were acting properly in showing a clear picture to George and Sally of the true significance of Christianity. They were not slaves to a given method but were sensitive servants of the Spirit.

If Rollingwood were more "Christianized" in the sense that greater numbers were in the problem-recognition stage (stage -3, Figure 3), it is likely that a saturation campaign of door-to-door witness might succeed. At this point, however, it is doubtful whether it would have much success. A better strategy would be to open avenues of communication in each neighborhood where Christian lay people get to know their neighbors both individually and in groups. In this way, they will actively assess spiritual status and tailor communication accordingly. Books and tapes, plus home evangelistic Bible studies, might prove successful. At the same time the mass media, such as radio, also will be functioning to stimulate interest and enhance the effectiveness of the personal witness.

Much insight can be gained from the wealth of studies done on the "diffusion of innovations."[20] One of the most interesting

---

[20] A vast literature is summarized in James F. Engel, David T. Kollat, and Roger D. Blackwell, *Consumer Behavior,* rev. ed. (New York: Holt, Rinehart and Winston, Inc., 1973), ch. 24. Also see the landmark volume by Everett M. Rogers and F. Floyd Shoemaker, *Communication of Innovations* (New York: Free Press, 1971).

findings is that new ideas often penetrate into a social setting as follows:

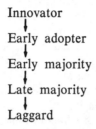

Innovator

Early adopter

Early majority

Late majority

Laggard

This suggests that some people (the innovators) are more prone to accept an innovation than others. Often these are the ones who are most exposed to the world outside of a specific social setting, particularly through the mass media. Once they accept the innovation, another group, the early adopters, will often follow along by accepting the example of the innovator. These are followed by the early majority, and so on. Most social settings will be characterized by people in each of these categories, and the greatest personal impact can be made first by reaching the innovator who then reaches others. Campus outreach, for example, logically begins with a focus on the campus leader, and the same can be done in an office, afternoon bridge club, or neighborhood softball team.

The Concept of the Media Mix

When more than one medium is utilized in a campaign, the combination is referred to as the "media mix." The net effect, in turn, is synergistic, the whole being greater than the sum of the parts. It has been suggested that the suburbanite commuter in Rollingwood in the twenty-five-to-forty age segment could be reached through a combination of spot radio announcements during driving time; cable television, if available; neighborhood Bible studies or other forms of friendship outreach; and lay witness, using a combination of books, magazines, cassettes, and personal testimony. The exact form that such a mix should take obviously varies substantially from one area to the next, the key determinant being the spiritual status of the audience. Note once again that door-to-door lay witness was not suggested for Rollingwood at this time, although it and other forms of persuasion such as evangelistic meetings might be very effective in a succeeding year if this campaign of proclamation suceeds as hoped.

In the final analysis, each media mix is unique, and the best form may be arrived at only through experience and experimentation. For example, it is known that street-corner meetings still work well with working-class people in urban areas in Brazil. Obviously, they should be utilized in a properly conceived evangelistic media mix. If there is doubt about any given medium, test it (or a combination of two or more) on a small scale over a short period of time and gauge the apparent response. For example, an evangelistic cassette tape should never be distributed until a few members of the target audience listen and give their response. This is a form of "pretesting" that may be very useful in helping to avoid a wrong decision.

In the final analysis, there never is one *best* media strategy. There probably are many combinations, all of which will work equally well. All that can be expected is that the combination of careful analysis and prayer will result in a program that is appropriate for the circumstances to be faced. Much will be learned that will permit a better performance in successive planning periods.

MEASUREMENT AND EVALUATION

The Lord has made it abundantly clear that His servants are to be accountable before Him for their labors. This means that we have no choice but to measure the effectiveness of our efforts and to evaluate the significance of what is learned for future planning.

The measurable goals given in Figure 4 now becomes absolutely essential, for measurement without such specificity is impossible. For instance, were the stated increases in awareness and attitude change actually achieved? The only way to find out is to undertake another survey in exactly the same form as the first and assess the changes that are observed. This type of testing is referred to quite logically as before-and-after measurement.[21]

If results fall short of the goal, it could signify that the goal was overly optimistic. If so, something has been learned. It also might be apparent that the strategy was deficient in certain respects. This, too, is valuable information for future planning. This is what is meant by the "post mortem" — examining the thing to see what made it die (or more optimistically, what made it live while it did). Try to assess what went well and what went wrong and then write it down for future reference! This information then becomes a part of experience that, as will be recalled, is one of those three essential bases of planning (along with intuition and research).

The post mortem also should assign responsibility for success and failure. Human beings seem to have a tendency to grab the credit while avoiding the blame. Again, this is a luxury we cannot take to ourselves, because God holds each person accountable. If we have failed in our performance, this may be a sure sign that we do not have the gift necessary for this function. To allow a brother or sister to continue to function in such fashion can hardly be called love. Rather, it is avoidance of our responsibility to God and to each other!

LOOKING BEYOND ROLLINGWOOD

For purposes of ease of communication and understanding, this chapter has been couched in terms of an admittedly hypothetical situation. Furthermore, only the most general overview of the steps in communication strategy could be given. Nevertheless, we have provided illustration of the steps necessary to design and implement a research-based, multiple-church, multiple-media strategy, regardless of where it is undertaken. The environmental analysis in Sao Paulo, Brazil, will be a far cry from that in Osaka, Japan, or Omaha, Nebraska, or wherever else one may be. The specific resulting strategies also will be greatly different. But the steps in analysis,

---

[21] This type of measurement is thoroughly discussed in Engel, Wales, and Warshaw, *Promotional Strategy,* ch. 14.

decision making, implementation, and evaluation are *always* the same. What we have been talking about is an approach to problem solving and we have carefully avoided suggesting a variety of strategies. Each strategy will be *unique* if we have done our planning properly.

Admittedly, the approach to planning suggested here is somewhat formalized. This is because proper attention must be paid to the all-important environmental research. Furthermore, the Holy Spirit seems to require this type of effort on our part (cf. Prov. 16:9). Without the options clearly thought through, how can He guide us? God has His specific ways of revealing His will in each generation, and it is always in keeping with the peculiar problems at hand.

The cooperative strategy has been stressed for the very reason that it lies at the heart of God's plan for our times. There are some precedents. The multiple-church evangelistic outreaches variously called "Evangelism in Depth," "Christ for All," or "New Life for All" have been undertaken throughout the world with generally good response. "Key '73" also had a measure of success in the United States. These are, of course, campaigns of persuasion designed mostly to generate decisions. In that sense, the strategy may not always fit the environment on which it is imposed. Nevertheless, it is our observation that the Holy Spirit is at work within the Church and its associated agencies to bring about a strong felt need for such integrative approaches in which firepower can be concentrated with greater results. The future may well lead all of us to put distinctive characteristics aside and unite in a greater sense of purpose to further that one great mission of the Church — world evangelization. In this sense, we may now be in the most exciting era in the history of the Church in which God's people together finish the work He placed us here to accomplish.

7

New Management

Acceptance of Christ signifies acceptance of *new management*. Old things pass away, and *all* things become new. But this does not occur all at once, because the new believer must be helped as he matures and grows in the image of Christ. Cultivation of the believer is also a part of the Great Commission; one does not automatically become a disciple overnight, A disciple is a *learner,* one who is in the process of finding true freedom in Christ. If you are a disciple, you are in the process of becoming that *one and only you.*[1] It is our purpose in the next two chapters to analyze this growth process and to uncover its implications for the Christian communicator.

THE "GOOD CHRISTIAN" STRAITJACKET

George and Sally Calderone have made that great discovery of knowing Jesus Christ personally. They are excited, enthusiastic, overflowing with new life.

They joined First Church, mostly through the influence of the Cranstons and the Richards. Church membership is necessary, because each believer must associate with others if he is to grow and mature in the faith. But they are about to face some unnecessary hurdles because a few well-meaning new

---

[1] *The One and Only You* (Waco, Texas: Word Books, 1973) is a challenging book by Bruce Larson who was used to help the first-named author and his wife to find freedom in Christ. This title captures, we feel, the essence of the Christian life.

friends will, without even realizing it, send them down some disastrous ways that are "deadends to growth."[2]

Squashed Into the Mold

Tom Bartlett dropped by one evening, as he often did, just to see how George and Sally were coming with their new life. After a time of prayer together, it was obvious to George that Tom had something else on his mind.

"George, I really hate to bring this up, but I think I had better do it. A few people have mentioned to me that they see you on the golf course early on Sunday morning."

"Sure, Pastor, but we still get to church," George interjected.

"I know that, George, and I'll admit it does seem kind of silly. Lots of Sundays I wish I could be out there with you. But you know how it is with some of our people. We always have to be careful not to do anything that would cause them to stumble."

As Tom walked out the door that night George couldn't help wondering what he had gotten himself into. *What's wrong with golf on Sunday?* he thought to himself.

It seems as if some cannot resist defining Christianity in terms of a list of "do's and don'ts." Many of these, of course, are biblical and hence should be taught to new believers as they mature to a point of understanding. But others, quite frankly, are cultural taboos that have been surrounded by high-sounding, stained-glass rationales and have become entombed into the lifestyle of the "good Christian" in many quarters.

And then there is that interesting point about "making others stumble." Paul rightly asserts in Romans 14:21 that the principle of love for a brother puts legitimate constraints on otherwise acceptable behavior: "It is good not to eat meat or to drink wine, or to do anything by which your brother stumbles." This is particularly true when the other person is weaker in the faith.

[2] See Keith Miller, *The Becomers* (Waco, Texas: Word Books, 1973), ch. 19.

But this great truth also may be used as a spiritual sledge-hammer to bludgeon others into conformity. After all, why should someone stumble over such things as dress styles, minor deviations in behavior, etc., when there is no clearcut violation of blibical principle?

The authors identify with the experience reported by Joe Bayly after he had timidly begun growing a beard. When confronted by the possibility that a "weaker brother" might stumble, Bayly said that those who might be offended are *not* weaker brothers. "I asked one if he was a weaker brother, and he was offended. I'm the weaker brother, and my fellow weaker brothers like my beard. It's the stronger brothers who object."[3]

But it's not only the "thou shalt nots" that can become a problem; it also is the "thou shalts." Some well-meaning Christians might say to George, "Now that you are a Christian, here are some things you will want to do:

1. Have a daily quiet time. It's best to do this in the morning. Try to read at least one chapter of the Bible.
2. Keep a prayer list for your unsaved friends. Pray for them daily.
3. Make witnessing a way of life. Every time you are with a person five minutes, consider this a divine appointment and seek ways to share Christ with him.
4. You should be in Sunday school, Sunday morning service, Sunday evening service, Wednesday evening prayer service, and Saturday morning men's prayer group. And, of course, that's just the beginning of the good things going on at church.
5. And be sure you get into Scripture memory. Five verses a week is a good start for a young Christian like you."

And on it goes. Here is a job description that becomes an impossibility! Obviously all of these things are good and will probably be present in one form or another in the life of most mature believers. But these good works emerge slowly through maturity and should never be imposed artificially. All too

---

[3] Joseph Bayly, *Out of My Mind* (Wheaton, Illinois: Tyndale House Publishers, 1970), p. 41.

often, this becomes just another form of legalism, which can squeeze the very joy out of the Christian life.

So here we have it — a kind of assembly line that produces one standard model of "good, orthodox, properly behaving, Bible-believing Christians." But somehow that first joy evaporates. Instead of the new-found freedom, the new Christian is forced into another mold, characterized mostly by an innocuous blandness. Where is the place for that person who dares to be different, who dares to shake the status quo (a Latin term meaning "the mess we is in"), and who dares to adopt the lifestyle of Jesus Christ in all that it means? Certainly not in the mold many of us have found in the church. Sadly, this mold is too often nothing but a caricature of the real thing. No wonder something has gone wrong with the harvest! Consider Bruce Larson's penetrating words:

> Now if God made each person to be unique, a one and only version of that life, then sin is expressed when internal and external forces cause us to lose our uniqueness and become a carbon copy, and usually a poor one, of another person or group. So the change that God offers is one that helps a person to find his true identity, his true personhood, and to become "the one and only you."[4]

Becoming a "Workaholic"

Yes, George and Sally are quickly becoming a part of the life at First Church. George, of course, is an advertising man, so guess who became head of the publicity committee? Also, an advertising man should know something about selling, so George and Sally were soon pressed into duty on the visitation committee. And, as happens to every new believer who has a "glamorous testimony," George was initiated into the Christian evangelistic banquet circuit. Pretty soon he covered the state from one end to the other, and everyone said he was a great blessing.

One week a very unusual thing happened. George and Sally were at home on a Friday night with nothing to do. "You

---

[4] Larson, *The One and Only You*, p. 38.

know, Honey," George said, "I feel guilty. All I want to do tonight is goof off, but I should be reading the Bible or something."

Welcome, George, to the world of the evangelical workaholics! George has succumbed to that insidious trap of Christian busyness. He always has been a "mover," a "doer," but it is the church's value system that is the real source of George's attitude. As a young believer, George shortly observed that some people at First Church were regarded as "better" Christians than others. Usually those were the ones who were "sacrificing for the kingdom" by their long hours of work. There is Ernie Randolph, for example, who won eight people to Christ last month. Al Cranston got a great pat on the back at the annual meeting for his untiring service, and it is true that Al is there at the church nearly every day. All of these things in themselves are fine, but "success" all too often becomes the measure of spirituality.

So now George is at the point where he feels guilty in "taking an evening off." What have we done but accentuate the chances that he will have the heart attack that seems to accompany his personality type. Is this the kind of lifestyle that Christ really wants? If so, why did He say to his disciples "Come away by yourselves . . . and rest a while?" (Mark 6:31). Why did both Ezra and Nehemiah rest for three days after their journeys from captivity in Babylonia back to Jerusalem?

The Christian workaholic is in bondage, working out of duty instead of love — make no mistake about that. And there is precious little joy! But how different was the life of Christ. He always walked; He never ran. He took time out for prayer, rest, refreshment, and even enjoyment. He never meant to substitute a new prison for the old prison of sin. Stephen Board wisely counsels that

> Christian discipleship does not call us to be always taut as a violin string with pious passion. Young Christians often think so and begrudge themselves the leisure, the hobbies, the humor that would make them seem more human and more real.[5]

---

[5] Editorial in *His* (May, 1974), p. 32.

Intellectualism

"George, my boy, if you want to grow in Christ, put doctrine into that frontal lobe."

So George began to dig into some pretty heavy stuff with great zeal at first. And he focused diligently on Tom Bartlett's sermons. The doctrine of justification, for example, was the subject of an eight-week sermon series. In the process of exposure he learned some valuable truths. But after a seemingly endless time of this, George woke up to the realization that he was bored stiff. "You know I can understand some of this," he told Tom, "but much of it just leaves me cold. I can't seem to figure out how it all applies to me."

George voiced what is on the mind of many in the pews who are struggling to grow in their faith. They are given doctrine, neatly packaged, and buttressed of course by the original languages. But it seldom touches their life. The problem is that genuine truth is often packaged in such a way that it is palatable only to a preacher's colleagues on the seminary level, and sometimes not even to them. Often it is not translated into categories meaningful to the layman. Nothing can be more dull and meaningless than doctrine presented at the fourteenth level of abstraction. Keith Miller provides the answer by noting that "a part of the current awakening in the church is that men and women are beginning to hear and speak about Christianity in the language and thought patterns of life — ordinary life."[6]

Our point, of course, is that biblical doctrine is foundational for growth, but its meaning emerges when it is focused in such a way that it is relevant to Christian experience. Growth in intellectual understanding does not signify maturity in and of itself; maturity comes when this doctrine is applied and utilized in day-to-day living.

The Resulting Caricature

We need to add a personal note here. Both of the authors, to one degree or another, have been directed into some of

---

[6] Miller, *The Becomers*, pp. 27, 28.

these dead ends to growth, plus others not mentioned here. But, more seriously, we have also been guilty of doing the same things to others. For example, one of us was diligently leading an "action group" of young Christians. This was composed of graduate students and faculty, nearly all of whom were new converts. The program consisted of training in various aspects of the Christian life, especially in face-to-face witness. Each week we went out two-by-two to talk with strangers in the dining hall and other places. The morale of the group surprisingly deteriorated until one blurted out, "Why don't you just bug off. What you are trying to do is create carbon copies of yourself in us, and I've had enough." That was the best thing that could have happened, because a certain type of "good Christian mold" indeed had been imposed on each one. The tragedy is that each person's uniqueness is thus suppressed and the resulting product is only a caricature of what Jesus promised. We must rethink what is really meant by a lifestyle *truly* conformed to the image of Christ.

THE REAL THING

A popular soft-drink jingle has been restated as "Christ — the real thing." There is profound truth in this phrase, but what, exactly is the "real thing" in the life of the believer? This will, of course, differ from one person to another, but there are some common properties.

The Lifestyle of Jesus Christ

The beatitudes contain the best summary of Jesus' own lifestyle, and He presented it as a model for believers throughout the ages. These are the qualities that should characterize the Christian (Matt. 5:3-11):

1. Poor in spirit — humble-minded without pride; God is given His rightful place at the center of life
2. Mourning — a genuine identification and oneness with God who imparts an ability to perceive the world as He does

3. Gentleness or meekness — a yielding of personal rights to God and a lifestyle that looks upon all possessions and attributes as a gift from God to be used for His glory
4. Hunger and thirst after righteousness — a healthy spiritual appetite for the Word of God and its application in ethical living
5. Merciful — forgiveness of those who offend and an attitude of love and understanding
6. Pure in heart — motives and desires under the control of God
7. Peacemakers — consistent lifestyle of making things right for those who have been wronged
8. Persecuted for righteousness' sake — so identified with the purposes of God that those who reject Him will also reject them

In every sense of the word, this type of lifestyle is the very antithesis of the world's standards, which enshrine "doing your own thing." Personal ambitions are subjugated to the will of God; self-seeking is never an objective; others are responded to with genuine love and acceptance.

At the end of his life the apostle John reflected on the attributes of the mature believer and boiled them down to just three essentials (1 John 2). First, "keep his commandments" (2:3). Whereas we do not come to Christ initially through any merit of good works, we are expected to *obey* Christ once we have accepted Him. Next, he is characterized by love — "The one who loves his brother abides in the light and there is no cause for stumbling in him" (2:10). And, finally, he will not be conformed to the world, "For all that is in the world, and the lust of the flesh and the lust of the eyes and the boastful pride of his life, is not from the Father, but is from the world" (2:16). Each of the eight qualities above can fit under these headings: (1) obedience — poor in spirit, hungering and thirsting after righteousness, being pure in heart; (2) love for the brothers — showing mercy, being a peacemaker; and (3) nonconformity to the world — mourning, gentleness, being persecuted for righteousness' sake.

If we attempt to cultivate the new believer by developing these properties, other things will fall into place. In the final analysis, these are the biblical principles of growth, which transcend cultural boundaries and limitations.

Setting Men Free

Let's return now to George and Sally in terms of the model of spiritual status we have used throughout the book (Figure 3). First, it is to be expected that each of them will experience some doubts immediately after the initial decision: "Was I really saved? Do I really have eternal life? What really happened? These doubts should be anticipated, and we have an obligation of immediate followup. The best strategy is simply to stress the biblical principle at each point, reaffirming the validity of the decision, identifying with the new Christian's doubts and anxiety, and helping him to bear this initial burden. The Word of God itself seems to suffice as the solution.

From here on, what should be done? Obviously, we cannot provide a manual for discipleship in these few pages, but there are a few points that should be stressed.

First, there is no question that a doctrinal foundation must be built. At a very minimum, initial teaching should center on the biblical perspective of the nature of man, the authority of the Word of God, and the uniqueness of Jesus. Furthermore, there are certain foundational behavior patterns that must be cultivated — confession of sin, the filling of the Holy Spirit, prayer, and so on.

How are such patterns best taught? Jesus' own example provides some clues. He seemed to feel that they were better "caught than taught." He spent His life developing twelve men, living with them day by day, and teaching from daily examples as they observed Him. Then these men were expected to develop the same qualities in others (2 Tim. 2:2). At least an element of this personal ministry can be recaptured through the small group in which the new believer is taken under the wing of a few others who truly care and assume responsibility for growth. Often others' observation of us teaches far more than our words.

Once this foundation is in place, true maturation begins. But it seems to take place most frequently in a largely unrecognized way — through failure! Bear in mind that it is the job of the Holy Spirit to conform the new believer to the image of Christ. Usually this will require exposure of certain patterns of behavior or thought that are *not* so conformed. As someone once put it, it is as if things seem to be going well and then an ugly hand comes up out of the muck saying, "Look at you." In short, the Spirit functions to bring about problem recognition throughout one's life — a recognition that "what is" falls short of "what ought to be." In this sense, failure is a perfectly normal part of growth. Yet all too often the fellowship of the church discourages anyone from expressing his failure. One of the authors once shared a problem with a well-known Christian leader only to receive the evaluation "Well, you just don't understand how to walk with God. Christians don't have those kinds of problems." No further conversation ensued at that point, and one young believer failed to receive the help he needed.

Needs are discovered through failure as the Holy Spirit brings about problem recognition. That does not imply *in any way* that the Christian life is not victorious. Victory comes by seeking biblical principles and applying them to our lives through faith. There is no justification for remaining in defeat by not going beyond problem recognition.

Remember the congregational analysis at First Church? It disclosed plenty of problems in the lives of the members, but most of the members were seeking solution. They were open to change! What an opportunity for Tom Bartlett and others to restore and build up that missing spiritual virility. People are seeking answers, but will we provide them?

Christians must have outlets to share these needs, and others in the body must assume the responsibility of showing them the biblical principles for solution. This requires a "two-fisted," practical kind of Christianity that builds spiritual muscle. Notice how different this is from the "good Christian straitjacket." Definite boundaries are placed on one's life by biblical principles, but, within the boundaries, he has the latitude to grow and develop his own uniqueness. George and Sally must be helped in this process by patient counseling, appropriate teaching, provision of books, and so on. The aim is to produce those eight qualities of the beautitudes in their lives, *over a lifetime,* as the Spirit of God works (Phil. 1:6).

Bill Gothard points out that God uses experiences and events in such a way as to "build his message into our lives." This, in turn, is the basis of that uniqueness that ministers to others as we reproduce the life of Christ. There are two dimensions in reproduction. First, there is a ministry in the Body of Christ through the use of spiritual gifts. Externally, spiritual reproduction is expressed through verbal and nonverbal witness to others — through day-to-day living as we follow Christ, seeking opportunities to share His love.

The stage of reproduction does not necessarily require great maturity, particularly in terms of the length of time one has been a Christian. Some new believers immediately begin to reproduce and share the light they have. Maturity brings about those all-important qualitative differences as one is simultaneously more sensitive to the needs of others and more receptive to the leading of the Spirit.

This process of being set free to follow the Spirit is not without its pitfalls. The believer needs real help along the way as problem recognition occurs and needs arise. Furthermore, there must be continual training in the fundamentals of the Christian life. All the time, great caution must be exerted to avoid putting out that spark of uniqueness through imposition of the "Christian pattern." The one great claim of Christianity is that it can produce people who "dare to be different." If this flame is snuffed, what exciting message do we have for the world?

At all costs, new Christians like George and Sally Calderone must be cultivated in such a way that they are involved on the active playing field. Far too many churches are composed of good Bible believing Christians who, for one reason or another, have taken their seat on the sidelines. Intermittent cheers echo, especially at big events, such as missionary conferences, but basically the church members are lined up in rows, wearing identical masks, with little to distinguish them from others. What a travesty this is when contrasted with the lifestyle Jesus expects!

What is the task of the Church? First, to understand the biblically revealed essentials of the Christian-growth process.

Next, to utilize a program of instruction and cultivation that meets people where they are, providing answers to *real* questions and thereby giving them the spiritual and intellectual equipment to move off the bench and onto the playing field. If this program is stripped of cultural impediments and focused on biblical fundamentals, perhaps once again we will return to an era when people will say of the Church, "The men who have turned the world upside down have come here, too."

8

Removing the Stone in the Shoe

In his lyrical fashion, Isaiah declared, "How lovely on the mountains are the feet of him who brings good news" (Isaiah 52:7). But feet are not so lovely if there is a stone in the shoe. Every step brings pain, and the necessary first act is to remove the stone.

In a real sense, the Christian growth process includes many occasions of the stone in the shoe: a problem of felt need, which must be ministered to. The purpose of the ministry of spiritual cultivation is to provide sound Bible-based help to keep Christians walking as disciples without having to cry "ouch" every time they take a step following the Lord.

The congregation analysis lifted the masks from those sitting in the pews at First Church and at the same time revealed that the stones in the shoes of so many had become so big that they had no choice but to sit on the bench. It hurt too much to do anything else.

"Don't ask me to share the Good News with those guys in my car pool, because they know I don't have any influence on that son of mine who just goes his own way."

"Why bother to read the Bible, because God hasn't really answered any of my prayers for years."

"What is this business about joy? I can barely bring myself to face each day, and it's for sure I can't take any more of this 'have-faith, everything-will-work-out' nonsense."

What explains the remarkable success of each of the following Christian ventures or phenomena: the *Living Bible,* the Bill Gothard Institute for Basic Youth Conflicts, and *The Taste of New Wine* by Keith Miller? Obviously, each of these and many others in its own way is making an impact on substantial numbers of people, and we could have listed many other things as well. What do they have in common? *Each, in its unique fashion, is scratching people where they itch.*

It seems remarkable to us how many critics within the Church have leveled their fire at various of the phenomena mentioned above. "The *Living Bible* is just a childrens' Bible" asserted a well-known theologian. "Miller doesn't 'proof text' those bold assertions." "Gothard just misuses Scripture, quoting it out of context." And on and on we go. Interestingly many of these same critics often continue to be safely ensconced in their pulpits or in their seminary classrooms. Sometimes some very different answers are arrived at when we assume the perspective of the man in the pew, of that layman who is struggling to find his "place to stand." Then it becomes less significant to dot the theological "i's" and cross the "t's" in precisely the "correct" manner.

Lest we be misunderstood, we *never condone* any form of corruption of biblical truth. Our plea at this point is to emerge from our "theological heavenlies" to that real world where the average garden variety of Christian lives. Take First Church as an example. It has 650 members. The congregational analysis disclosed, as one might expect, that many points of problem recognition are shared in common — family, Bible reading, need for meaningful Christian relationships, spiritual gifts, and so on. Therefore, it is possible to develop a strategy of cultivation that will meet the needs of larger segments while, simultaneously, ministering to each individual within the segment. The very same thing can be said for any of the variety of church-related communication agencies such as publishers and broadcasters. The starting point always is analysis of the audience for purposes of developing an effective adaptive strategy of cultivation that scratches where they itch.

PRYING UNDER THE MASK

As was pointed out in chapter 1, most of those good First Church members seemed to wear a mask that says, "I'm fine; no problems." But surveys now show that this *is* just a facade that usually covers some deep and often ugly hurts. Now and again someone takes the mask off only to be told that "good Christians don't have those kinds of problems." As a result, either that person drops out to find something authentic outside the walls of the institution or he too learns how to use the mask. The only problem is that these hurts become repressed and more and more internalized until the point is reached where all real spiritual vitality and joy are stifled.

To begin to deal with the problem, we must first pry under the mask. If the Church is a true community of believers characterized by genuine face-to-face interaction, this may not be too difficult. John Wesley, for example, required his flock to attend a weekly class meeting that had an interesting agenda. Each was expected to live up to Christian standards, and all those in the group assumed real responsibility for each other. This included both encouragement and admonition. Furthermore, if one did not attend the class meeting, he didn't get his ticket to come to the Sunday morning service. Now, in such circumstances, will there be many pew sitters with stones in their shoes? Obviously not.

What happens, however, when there are hundreds in the flock? It is here that it becomes possible to wear the mask, and the absence of true community on a face-to-face basis makes it virtually impossible to assess where the other person is spiritually. This is accentuated by program orientation that does not adapt programs to the people. After all, how can they be adapted to if we don't have information?

There are some attempts, of course, to break through and discover real needs. Tom Bartlett, for example, always asks in the Sunday services whether anyone has a prayer request. "Yes, Nellie Townsend had surgery Thursday and is at County Hospital." "The Andersons had to fly home; her mother is ill." There are always these kinds of requests, which are significant and legitimate. But does anyone ever stand up and say, "I'd just like to praise God today because of what He taught me in . . . . . ."? Or "I need your prayers, because for some reason I just feel depressed. It has hung on for days, and I can't figure it out." No, such personal things seem to have no place in our churches today. No wonder our services have a tendency to become tasteless and ineffective!

The Survey

Probably the only way to get behind the masks in such circumstances is to use some type of survey. There is no magic in the survey instrument per se. It is only a tool that is proving useful worldwide in gathering information. Let's keep our eye on the fact that *information is gathered for purposes of planning.* Surveys are never an end in themselves. This may seem completely obvious to the reader, but we find that church leaders often become enamored with the survey and lose sight of its ultimate purpose. This is a real Satanic trap.

Now, with this warning behind us, how can a survey be used? The first purpose of a survey is to assess the level of doctrinal understanding. This does not require a multiple-choice quiz on such things as the order of the books of the Bible or completion sentences such as "The story of God giving Moses the Ten Commandments appears in . . . ." Memory, in and of itself, is of little basic relevance. The key is to discover whether or not there is a grasp of the fundamental aspects of the Christian faith. Some of the more important topics would include confession of sin, the filling of the Spirit, the meaning of the Body of Christ, spiritual gifts, the practical power of prayer, and so on.

Is the believer equipped to take his or her place both in the Body of Christ and in the world? If not, some real clues are provided for strategy. At First Church, for example, most have not witnessed to others in the past month, and the majority indicated a desire for training in how to relate the Christian message to nonbelievers. Obviously, some type of training program should be instituted, especially since this is a high priority among felt needs.

The second area of information is the *lifestyle of the believer.* We have seen the importance of lifestyle in the earlier discussion in chapter 6. The inquiry focuses on basic activities, interests, and opinions to discover sources of motivations and felt needs. Figure 5 contains some examples of this type of questioning selected from a survey that was taken among Christians in the country of Brazil. This project, by the way, is a cooperative venture of the Wheaton Graduate School, Overseas Crusades, and Bethany Fellowship. Its pur-

	This Is Me			This Is Not Me		
I tend to worry too much that we won't have all the money we need.	☐	☐	☐	☐	☐	☐
Children take up so much of my time that I don't have much time for anything else.	☐	☐	☐	☐	☐	☐
I really am not as concerned as I should be about the needs of my non-Christian neighbors.	☐	☐	☐	☐	☐	☐
I like to watch or listen to football games.	☐	☐	☐	☐	☐	☐
I think I have more confidence in myself than most of the other people I know.	☐	☐	☐	☐	☐	☐
No matter how hard I try, there are some people I just cannot love.	☐	☐	☐	☐	☐	☐
I buy things on credit.	☐	☐	☐	☐	☐	☐
I would like to take a trip around the world.	☐	☐	☐	☐	☐	☐
People often look to me for advice about things that concern them.	☐	☐	☐	☐	☐	☐
I feel pretty sure I can do almost anything I really want to do.	☐	☐	☐	☐	☐	☐
Praying together as a family is a part of my home life.	☐	☐	☐	☐	☐	☐
My children are the most important thing in my life.	☐	☐	☐	☐	☐	☐
I am convinced that birth control devices lead to sinful sexual behavior.	☐	☐	☐	☐	☐	☐
I often help the needy.	☐	☐	☐	☐	☐	☐
There are times when I feel very lonely.	☐	☐	☐	☐	☐	☐
I have close non-Christian friends with whom I share my feelings and concerns.	☐	☐	☐	☐	☐	☐
I would be in favor of trying some new forms of worship in my church.	☐	☐	☐	☐	☐	☐

Figure 5. Analysis of Spiritual Lifestyle

pose is to uncover the needs of various segments of Christians located in and adjacent to the major metropolitan areas of Brazil. The data then will be utilized in the development of new books and other forms of literature realistically *adapted* to the audience.

A third concern is attitudinal evaluation of the organization undertaking the survey; e.g., the local congregation, the magazine, the radio station, and so on. In other words, what image does the audience have of the church (or other organization) in terms of the degree to which the program offered meets their own unique needs? Tom Bartlett was floored to discover that nearly 50 percent stated they were not being "fed spiritually" at First Church for the reasons brought out elsewhere in the congregational analysis. If it did nothing else, this evidence served to jolt him into a state of problem recognition.

Finally, an attempt should be made to obtain an inventory of actual Christian behavior, especially in such sensitive areas as evangelistic witness, expression of social concern, the gathering together with other believers, and so on. This should be coupled with an assessment of felt need for change.

Most of those in First Church are not presently involved in evangelistic witness, but they are concerned about this shortcoming. On the other hand, there is less concern that the church is doing little to meet the social needs of the community. A program in evangelistic training will be well received, but quite the opposite is likely to be experienced if social concern becomes a priority emphasis. What should the church do?

One of the authors for a period of years was engaged in a ministry to encourage faculty members on the secular campus to become more involved in evangelistic outreach. In particular, the need for a verbal witness to students was stressed in a variety of ways. Only a handful were found to engage in such outreach, and it was discovered that the vast majority did not evidence a need for change. The program had little effect on the majority, but the smaller group already recognizing a need did respond, and some have had quite remarkable ministries.

What this illustrates is that comparatively little will be accomplished if there is not a recognized need for change.

Preaching and admonition fall mostly on closed filters. *But this does not mean that the prophetic ministry of the Church should be concluded.* There is no justification for bland toleration of shortcomings within a body of believers. The expectation should be that the Holy Spirit will work through the ministry of sanctification to open the filters and bring about problem recognition where the need is legitimate. Perhaps only a minority will respond, but this should not be viewed as a limitation.

The Publisher and the Broadcaster

Now, looking beyond the local church for a moment, we have undertaken a number of surveys at the Wheaton Graduate School for Christian magazines and radio stations. Often the data are unmistakably clear — only a minority out there are listening or reading. A survey for a teenage Christian magazine was especially revealing. The main articles were on the subjects of suffering, church performance, and Christian marriage. Each was read by only 20 percent of those who received the publication — a disturbingly low level of readership. Why do you think this happened? Most readers can quickly supply the answer, and it lies in the fact that this magazine was discussing issues that were nowhere near the minds of these kids. Those surveyed indicated that their main interests are school, dating, clothes, etc.; their principal problems lie in brother-sister relationships, relationships with parents, appearance, sex and dating, and school. So here you have it — the teenage readers were moving in one direction and the magazine in another. The editorial staff took these data seriously and greatly revamped the magazine content. The result has been a notable increase in readership, accompanied by other signs that real help is being provided in coping with the issues of life.

In another situation, it was discovered that only two of six major Christian radio programs received any meaningful share of the audience of a radio station that offers a mixture of Christian and secular programming. Upon closer analysis, it was determined that these programs spoke uniquely to the needs and interests of significant segments within the overall audience. The remainder attracted only a tiny minority of listeners with little or no discernible impact on their lives. Some substantial revamping is called for in programming philosophy and strategy.

As a final illustration, let us consider the *African Challenge* — a magazine published by the Sudan Interior Mission. In recent years it has been experiencing difficulties stemming from a series of adverse circumstances, and it became apparent that further publication was unwarranted unless it could be demonstrated that the periodical truly was playing a role in cultivating the believer.[1] A survey was undertaken in a number of churches by the Communication Center of the mission to disclose, among other things, personal needs and specifically Christian needs. The four most frequently mentioned personal problems were education, occupation, marriage/family/home and money. And a number of issues related to practical aspects of Christian behavior were unearthed. This led to the conclusion that the periodical should be renamed and positioned to speak pointedly to the following issues:

1. What is appropriate behavior for Christians in the Nigerian urban society?
2. How can a Christian experience more fully the inner reality and power that God has available for him?
3. How can one know whether he is really born again; what can he do about it; and what will be the consequences in terms of life experience in Nigeria?

And these issues should be viewed through the window of the target's perception of the problem.[2]

Where Do We Start?

A carefully designed survey, then, can be of real value in prying off the Christian mask. Many church leaders immedi-

---

[1] Donald Miller, "How to Publish in Nigeria for Nominal Christians in Churches" (mimeographed report, Sudan Interior Mission Communication Center, May, 1973).

[2] Ibid., p. 53.

ately would agree, but how does one begin? There are several church-related agencies that can be of help here. Of greatest significance thus far is the church-planning service provided by In-Depth Evangelism Associates (IDEA), a ministry of the Latin American Mission, Inc., located in Miami, Florida. The IDEA congregational survey is only a beginning step in arriving at a strategy adapted to the unique circumstances of each church. Again, the focus is on *planning,* not on a survey or on a particular program. Similarly, the revised "Way of Life Plan" offered by the Lay Ministry of Campus Crusade for Christ utilizes a congregational survey to uncover unmet needs.[3] Some churches also have utilized the Church Data Bank provided by the David C. Cook Company in Elgin, Illinois, although the emphasis here is on data collection rather than on the uses of the data by the congregation. Other sources also could be mentioned if space allowed.

Publishers and broadcasters, on the other hand, usually must tailor their own inquiry to their own unique audience. There are various research organizations that can be of help, although it is becoming increasingly apparent that a research department should be a part of any Christian communication organization, no matter how small. Excellence in production or graphics means little if content is missing the mark with the audience. The secular communicators discovered this fact *thirty years ago.* Why must the Christian organization so often play the role of a follower rather than a leader?

THE STRATEGY OF CULTIVATION

A strategy to cultivate the believers requires precisely the same type of managerial approach as that discussed in chapter 6. Briefly, the starting point is analysis of the environment, especially the audience, followed by establishment of goals, determination of program (message and media), measurement of effectiveness, and evaluation.

One possible goal for First Church would be as follows: "to

[3] Wanda Sorensen, "A Way of Life for Dynamic Church Growth: The Way of Life Plan," *Worldwide Impact* (May, 1974), pp. 27-29.

motivate 50 percent to be actively involved in evangelistic witnessing and to respond affirmatively to the statement 'Within the past month I have tried to lead a non-Christian to faith in Jesus Christ.' " Related to this, a secondary goal could be "to have 80 percent respond affirmatively to the statement 'I feel able to talk confidently with a non-Christian about faith in Jesus Christ.' " These goals, of course, focus on only one area of demonstrated need; there would also have to be similar specific statements pertaining to Bible reading, family devotions, body life, and so on.

Once again, it is worth restating that it really is not possible to determine strategy without well-thought-out goals. It is not always possible to state goals in precise quantitative terms, but a serious attempt should be made to do so. For example, it is apparent that the new goals for the *African Challenge* magazine, although not quantitative in statement, are precise and useful.

What might happen if goals were stated for each sermon or Sunday school lesson. A speaker, for example, had the purpose of communicating just one point: "One purpose for prayer is for you to get God's perspective on your situation; make this your aim the next time you pray." Now this is a simple enough point isn't it? When various of the hearers said, "I enjoyed your sermon," he asked, "What did you enjoy about it?" He probed to ascertain that this main theme had been registered. In further conversations later in the week, he also attempted to discover the experience of the hearers as they applied what he had said.

The Message

Tom Bartlett, in a recent sermon, interjected, "If you will excuse a personal illustration — " and then proceeded to comment briefly about an incident in his own family. Much to his surprise, some of those who had appeared to be dozing snapped to attention. It is as if their filters were suddenly allowing something to get through.

What happened here? Tom had been taught in seminary that personal illustrations should be used with great discretion, if at all. Maybe such a rule was relevant for another era, but not today. One of the great problems of men and women all over the world today is loneliness, leading to depersonalization and a sense of meaninglessness. People are seeking real answers, not abstract doctrine.

In the final analysis, if Tom cannot make personal applications of any given subject, then perhaps he should not be preaching on it. To preach most effectively on a topic, one must live it. That is, he must have some personal, experiential knowledge of his subject; otherwise, he is an "empty cymbal or a clanging gong." There is something compelling in the "power of the personal."

The personal application, of course, is not an end in itself. The purpose is to make biblical truth live, no matter how it is presented. Our point here is that this becomes mighty difficult if the writer or speaker has not walked that mile and is not willing to be sufficiently vulnerable to share his inner feelings and strivings.

Another key to effective communication is to avoid the trap of developing a jargon that merely becomes the "in-group" language of the church. The communicator has an obligation to employ terms that are meaningful to the reader or hearer in terms of his background and lifestyle.

Finally, every effort should be made to separate biblical truth from the cultural trapping. This is especially critical in communicating with those in other cultures. As we have stressed repeatedly, what is appropriate for a conservative midwestern North American context may be totally inappropriate and even destructive when presented indiscriminately elsewhere. For example, in one country, the "first point" is always attributed to Satan. So a sermon that stresses the "first point" is likely to wind up producing results far different from what was intended. An entire volume could be written on the subject of crosscultural communication alone.

Bear in mind that this warning is also valid within the United States. Conservative theology and conservative politics, for example, have traditionally been intermingled in evangelical ranks. Yet, there is a growing group of evangelicals of all ages who strongly argue against such an intermixture and who will, if anything, be negatively influenced if strictly biblical and strictly cultural positions are not separated.[4] From all indications, the numbers of those in these ranks appear to be growing rapidly.

Other than these few cautions, there are no guidelines for construction of the message. Each situation is unique, and, as was emphasized in chapter 6, the search for general rules has proved fruitless, even in the secular world.[5] There is no substitute for experience and research.

The Media

A variety of media is useful in the cultivation of the believer. But once again we must stress that the generalizations presented here are simply that — generalizations. There can be some real differences between segments within a single country and certainly from one country to another. The best media mix is arrived at by research, although some general guidelines are always useful.

The Sermon. The sermon, without doubt, is the mainstay of the evangelical church. Every community has some churches that draw larger crowds than others simply because of the oratorical ability of the preacher. No wonder homiletics receives such emphasis in the seminary. And Christian periodicals continue to boom out with the great proclamation that "What this country needs more than anything else is a return to great preaching!" There certainly is plenty to be said for that.

But, at the same time, with fear and trembling, we must raise a question in the light of the principles of communication: *Is this emphasis on the sermon really biblical?*

Maybe it is time to rethink the primacy we have placed on the sermon. Does it represent a biblical constant that should be retained, or is it a variable that should change as condi-

---

[4] See Richard Quebedeaux, *The Young Evangelicals* (New York: Harper & Row, 1974).

[5] See, for example, Leo Bogart, *Strategy in Advertising* (New York: Harcourt, Brace, and World, Inc., 1967).

tions change? Gavin Reid suggests that it is a variable, and there is much to support this view.[6]

There was a time, especially after the Reformation, when the pastor was the only educated member of the congregation. The hunger for the Word of God had to be met somehow, and the most logical method was through the spoken message delivered by a learned man of the cloth. But times changed. Bibles rapidly became available at low cost, and growing numbers acquired the education they previously lacked. It now has reached the point where many in a congregation are as well-educated as the pastor, or possibly better-educated than he is, and some are probably equally well-equipped to teach, even though they don't have a seminary degree.

Times have changed in yet another crucial respect. In an earlier era, a highly structured message consisting of a few main points followed by a logical conclusion was quite appropriate. Today we would refer to this as a "hot message"[7] — highly structured and leading to an unmistakable and well-articulated conclusion. The post–World War II era, however, is the television age. The majority of those who are now alive have been influenced by that unique combination of sight and sound — a montage of stimuli that involve the viewer in a much less structured way. In other words, the "cool message" has become more commonplace, and today's generation is not as responsive as its predecessors to the "hot" approach epitomized by the typical sermon.

Given these basic social changes, then, is the sermon — the lecture — still required in the church service? Probably in the final analysis this question must be answered at the level of the individual congregation. Many, particularly those under the age of thirty-five, may respond more strongly to some other

---

[6] Gavin Reid, *The Gagging of God* (London: Hodder and Stoughton, 1969), especially chs. 1-5.

[7] McLuhan has claimed that media themselves are hot or cool. (See Marshall McLuhan and Quentin Fiore, *The Medium Is the Message* (New York: Bantam Books, 1970). We disagree, however, because one cannot separate the message from the medium. Message structure is the most important variable. For elaboration see James F. Engel, Hugh G. Wales, and Martin R. Warshaw, *Promotional Strategy*, 3rd ed. (Homewood, Illinois: Richard D. Irwin, Inc., 1975), ch. 13.

type of presentation, particularly if use is made of visual aids, creative worship styles, and so on. Others who have grown up with the sermon probably cannot live without it.

But in a more fundamental sense, could our reliance on the sermon, in itself, be a reason that so many churches are composed largely of Sunday-morning-only Christians? Perhaps we have built the expectation that everything centers around the worship service. Come, listen, and leave. Maybe now is the time for change, or at least for experimentation in other forms.

Each church must assess the extent to which the sermon is accomplishing its intended purpose of building the believer. There is nothing absolute about it. The biblical ministry of preaching and teaching can be expressed in a multitude of other ways.

Christian Education. Somehow the church has a responsibility to teach the believer, and Sunday school is the time-honored way, at least in the United States. Typically Sunday school does not meet before 9:30 on a Sunday morning (after all, the cows must be milked first) and it consists of opening exercises followed by from thirty to forty-five minutes of teaching that utilizes materials prepared by a denomination or major publisher. The usual approach to teaching, in turn, is a lecture followed by from three to five minutes of discussion. And then we are through.

Modern education, on the other hand, is stressing some different approaches. The lecture is supplemented or even replaced by a variety of audio-visual media. And content certainly is not put forth in a dogmatic fashion. Students are taught to think, and rarely is emphasis placed on the one "right answer" to controversial questions. Far more important is development of an ability to think. Finally, learning is an interaction between student and teacher, with primacy placed on individual expression.

All too often, the Sunday school is the exact antithesis of secular education. Dogmatic answers are given ("Don't challenge the Bible!"). But if the Bible won't withstand honest scrutiny, what good is it? Furthermore, students of all ages tend to chafe in a lecture situation where their individuality either is quashed or not given opportunity for expression.

We are pleased to note, however, that dramatic change is taking place in Christian education.[8] New approaches and new materials abound. Furthermore, it is no longer confined to the Sunday morning time slot and is finding expression in the home, at camps, in small groups, etc.

Unfortunately, progress in Christian education is still largely confined to North America, with one significant exception — theological education by extension. In many quarters of the world the church has no education ministry other than a Sunday sermon, but thousands of leaders have recently been trained through programmed instruction and other means. This signals a great step forward.

Books. Literature has always been among the most significant media for building the believer. Sales of evangelical books increased over 14 percent in the United States during 1974, and the upward trend continues both here and abroad. In fact, one can hardly keep up with the new titles.

Yet we must interject a sobering note into this otherwise bright picture. What, exactly, is being accomplished by this plethora of books? Many books are virtual carbon copies of others, as witnessed, for example, by the nest of titles on the return of Christ written from a dispensational point of view. Only a handful attain a substantial sales volume, and rarely do we center our inquiry on the *effects* on the individual.

Some books, as was mentioned earlier, are unquestionably meeting genuine, demonstrated need. Others seem to attain relatively large sales volumes more through advertising muscle than through any real merit. The publishing business is unusual in one respect. Most books are written in the hopes that they will succeed, and careful research rarely enters into the decision to write and to publish. No wonder the situation is so spotty in terms of impact.

The situation becomes more serious outside of North America. Many books published elsewhere are translations of American titles. Those who are responsible are among the first to admit that they have little objective basis for a publishing

---

[8] See, especially, Lawrence Richards, *A New Face for the Church* (Grand Rapids: Zondervan Publishing House, 1970). Also Kenneth O. Gangel, *Leadership for Church Education* (Chicago: Moody Press, 1970).

decision, to say nothing of an understanding of the real effects of a given title in a ministry of cultivation. Usually it is a matter of monitoring American sales and translating those titles that appear to be "hot." What this means, of course, is that some needs of the Christian market are met, whereas others go completely neglected.

The only final basis for decisions to publish or not to publish is a continual monitoring of the needs of various segments of the reading public, followed by development of appropriate titles. This is precisely the strategy that is followed by Pioneer Girls, Inc., of Wheaton, Illinois, in the development of the new curriculum for discipleship of schoolage girls in churches. The study of Christians in Brazil referred to earlier was undertaken for exactly the same final purpose — to develop books that will make a demonstrable difference in the lives of believers.

Magazines. The magazine or other form of periodical can be considered in much the same manner as were books in the above discussion. There is an advantage, however, in that a known audience subscribes, and it is relatively simple to monitor this audience periodically to determine their current needs and opinions. Thus, there is no excuse to "fly in the dark" with respect to editorial content. The study of *African Challenge* is an ideal illustration.

Audio Cassettes. In many parts of the world, people either cannot read or cannot afford to purchase any form of literature. In these instances, in particular, the audio cassette performs an invaluable service. It can be tailored to speak to issues precisely and in the language of those for whom it is intended. Complete programs of Bible study can be included, for example. This has been done with great success in Thailand and elsewhere. How else can excellent teaching be carried into areas where the local pastor has not progressed beyond a primary education?

The cassette has an equally valuable function in the more developed society, however. Because of its versatility, the tape player can be utilized while the listener is doing other things. In this sense, "time can be used twice." The growing popularity of tape ministries attests to the significance of this medium in the life of the believer.

Cable Television. Largely a United States phenomenon as yet, cable television is opening new opportunities for the church as was pointed out initially in chapter 6. In the context of this chapter, cable offers great promise as a teaching medium. The very best teachers and programs of all types may be captured inexpensively on video cassette and then played for viewing in the home, at neighborhood Bible studies, etc. The opportunity is increasingly recognized, but the great need now is for *quality* material that may be purchased by, or loaned to, a local group for airing in this manner.

Christian Radio. Last, we come to that uniquely American medium — Christian radio. While there are missionary radio stations in all quarters of the globe, the presence of a Christian broadcasting station in nearly all major markets is largely confined to the United States. Today there are approximately three hundred Christian stations on both the AM and the FM dials, and there are additionally hundreds of groups that supply the various programs. In fact, it is reported by the National Religious Broadcasters that during 1972 an average of one new station was opened each week.

Thousands of Christians will attest to the significance of the teaching ministry received over the radio. Some long-standing programs truly have become household mainstays in Christian homes. The effects of this ministry never should be underestimated.

Nevertheless, in spite of the unquestioned value of Christian radio, we cannot help being concerned about many of the stations operating in America. We don't mean to be uncharitable when we point out that there is money to be made in Christian radio. Not surprisingly, there are frequent announcements in *Advertising Age* or *Broadcasting* that another secular station is about to go religious in its format because of the profit opportunity. It is all too easy to substitute profit for ministry. This, of course, is also true of Christian publishing or any other form of Christian business.

Perhaps the more basic question centers on the return for the investment placed in Christian radio. Only a handful of stations or program producers have any objective measure of their listening audience, and rarely is it found by published syndicated radio ratings that those who are listening to radio at any given time exceed 5 percent of the population. Further-more, the bulk of listeners are females fifty years of age or older.[9] Does this type of audience justify the investment necessary to maintain a Christian station, to say nothing of producing the plethora of programs? This question is rarely, if ever, raised in Christian broadcasting circles, but it must be addressed. The fact is that a strong case could be made for placing the same resources in audio or video cassettes with the expectation of producing greater effects in the lives of the listeners.

As asserted earlier, it is no longer warranted to maintain the Christian station (i.e., with programs of preaching, teach-ing, and hymns) on the assumption that through it the un-saved will be evangelized. Although conversions will, of course happen, they are the exception rather than the rule.[10] Chris-tian programs tend to draw an already-Christian audience! The issue to be decided, then, is whether or not the effects on the believer warrant the current level of investment of limited resources. Obviously, this must be decided at the level of each individual station or with respect to an individual program: Who is being reached with what effect? Objective answers are demanded, not just opinions!

Measurement of Effectiveness

In chapter 6, the measurement of effectiveness was dis-cussed thoroughly, and it will be recalled that some type of before-and-after measurement will often be required. First Church, for example, stated the evangelistic training goals that were cited earlier in that chapter. After the program has been executed for a year (or for a shorter or longer period, depending on planning needs), an identical survey should be taken to assess the changes that have occurred in the interim. Were the goals attained or not?

---

[9] See, for example, *Family Radio News* (July/August/Septem-ber, 1974), p. 3, which documents precisely this point.

[10] This is the common conclusion from analysis of mail response to the Christian station. As a result, such leaders as WMBI in Chicago forthrightly state their ministry to be one of cultivation.

The publisher and broadcaster have a somewhat different type of research inquiry. This consists of monitoring the audience to determine who is reading or listening and what is happening in their lives as a result. Such research is routine in the non-Christian world, and it is now seen here and there among Christian publishers in particular. The broadcasters, on the other hand, seem to be more content to operate without this information, although there are some exceptions, of course.

What should one say about a Christian radio station that claims to be reaching five million people and urges listeners to "give another hundred dollars to reach another one hundred people"? Usually this type of appeal is based on the fact that there are that stated number of people in the potential geographical area to be covered. But it is something else to claim that they will be, in fact, both reached *and* influenced through proclamation, persuasion, or cultivation. This kind of assertion wouldn't be tolerated for a minute in the secular world, which insists upon objective measures of accountability. The potential donor simply should ask, "Show me the facts — who is being reached with what effect?" We must not tolerate nonverified claims that are nothing more than deception, even though deception undoubtedly is not the intent. God asks far more of us than this in terms of our stewardship.

To Sum It Up —

Analyze the environment, set goals, prepare an adaptive strategy, and measure effectiveness. We seem to have a stuck record, but what other answer is there? The purpose is to help believers grow to maturity in Christ. There is no excuse for a body of believers to go hobbling around because of that stone in the shoe.

PART IV

The Adaptive Strategy and the Local Church

We have now explored the implications of the Great Commission in a twentieth-century world and have seen that a successful ministry of proclamation, persuasion, and cultivation requires careful spirit-led analysis, planning, strategy, and measurement. This will go far toward the objective of restoring the missing cutting blades. But one all-important consideration yet remains — will the Church be characterized by resistance to change or by renaissance?

There is no question that the Church is God's only means for accomplishing His work on earth.[1] Other organizations such as evangelistic movements, broadcasters, publishing agents, and mission societies are best considered "parachurch structures," which exist alongside of and parallel to the community of God's people.[2] Although they are helpful in carrying out its purposes, they are *not* the Church. There is nothing in their mandate that imparts a divine guarantee of permanent existence to them. In fact, one can make the case that these groups could diminish both in size and importance if they are succeeding in stimulating and assisting the Church in performing the functions that, by divine decree, belong solely to it.

Unfortunately, the church in most quarters today is in an effectiveness crisis. Of course, we acknowledge the *many* exceptions to this generalization, but this does not negate the fact that First Church of Rollingwood is all too typical of those churches that characterize themselves as evangelical. Churches in the liberal camp that deny the basic historic fundamentals of the Christian religion have deteriorated even further to the point of an effectiveness *calamity.* The 1974 *Yearbook of*

---

[1] Howard A. Snyder, "The Church as God's Agent of Evangelism" in *Let the Earth Hear His Voice,* official ref. vol. of the International Congress on World Evangelization, ed. J. D. Douglas (Minneapolis: World Wide Publications, 1975) pp. 327-60.

[2] Ibid.

Churches documents the slide of some of these close to oblivion.

Church history also reveals some sobering lessons. When the Church retrenches into a static policy of resistance to change, it becomes a mere empty shell. The exterior trappings may appear adequate, but the interior vitality has long since expired. This, of course, is typical of a church in effectiveness crisis — going on, business as usual. But then a renaissance occurs — a breakthrough of the Holy Spirit, a new birth of relevance! All too often this new wine cannot be contained in the old wineskins and a new fellowship must be formed. At other times, the new life has infected the "empty" shell itself, reversed the effectiveness slide, and restored the body to its true function.

There is no point in talking about fulfillment of God's mission if the Church is entombed in resistance. The answer does not lie in renewal of old forms, because that often is an attempt only to place band-aids on the exterior wounds of the old shell. The key is renaissance — a rebirth in the Body of Christ, locally and worldwide.

The key, we feel, lies in the discovery of the *principles* of New Testament church organization and function. The particular expression of these principles in the first century, however, should be viewed only as a historical record of those forms appropriate to that environment. It makes little sense to impose this cultural expression on the Church today, because that is just another form of program orientation. Fortunately, God has led many to search for these principles and to apply them creatively.[3]

---

[3] Of particular value, we feel, are the following: Lawrence Richards, *A New Face for the Church* (Grand Rapids, Michigan: Zondervan Publishing House, 1970); Orlando E. Costas, *The Church and Its Mission: A Shattering Critique From the Third World* (Wheaton, Illinois: Tyndale House Publishers, Inc., 1974); David Mains, *Full Circle* (Waco, Texas: Word Books, 1971); Robert Raines, *New Life in the Church* (New York: Harper & Row, 1961); Elizabeth O'Connor, *Call to Commitment* (New York: Harper & Row, 1963); Elton Trueblood, *The Incendiary Fellowship* (New York: Harper & Row, 1967); Robert C. Girard, *Brethren, Hang Loose* (Grand Rapids: Zondervan Publishing House, 1972); and C. Peter Wagner, *Look Out! The Pentecostals Are Coming* (Carol Stream, Illinois: Creation House, 1973).

9

The Church:
Resistance or Renaissance?

If one were to stop at a gas station in Rollingwood and ask directions to First Church, the attendant no doubt would answer by giving the address of the church building. This is the common conception that identifies the Church with the visible institutional structure.

The Bible takes quite a different view. The visible manifestation is not even mentioned. Instead, the Church is viewed as the Body of Christ — the true laity or people of God (1) organized under one Head, Jesus Christ; (2) equipped by God to perform His functions; (3) ministering to each other; (4) ministering to the world; (5) characterized by a lifestyle of obedience; and (6) reproducing itself individually and corporately.

WHAT IS THE CHURCH?
A Body Organized Under One Head

The apostle stated for all time that Christians "are no longer strangers and aliens, but you are fellow-citizens with the saints, and are of God's household, having been built upon the foundation of the apostles and prophets, Christ Jesus Himself being the cornerstone, in whom the whole building, being fitted together, is growing into a holy temple in the Lord" (Eph. 2:19-21). And Christ is given as "head over all things to the church, which is His body, the fulness of Him who fills all in all" (Eph. 1:22, 23).

137

The Church, then, in its biblical essence is a live, functioning organism. It may or may not have a building. In fact, the very erection of a building all too quickly can divert focus from the true nature of the Church and focus it instead on the building itself and the actions therein. This "edifice complex" is often one of the most significant manifestations of advanced effectiveness crisis.

How does the Church function under the control of the Head, Jesus Christ, when He is not physically present on earth? There must be avenues for communication, one of which is prayer. Prayer, properly conceived, indeed *is* two-way communication in which praise and adoration and petitions are made to God through the Lord Jesus Christ, *and answers are received.* Furthermore, specific guidance and direction are received from the Holy Spirit, who will "guide you into all the truth" (John 16:13). Consequently, Christ truly could say to His disciples with respect to His good works, that they would do "greater works than these" (John 14:12).

Worship is yet another means of communication that, quite frankly, is often misunderstood and misused by the Church. The typical 11:00 A.M. worship service is a curious phenomenon. While formats vary, most follow this kind of pattern: announcements, hymn, Scripture reading, prayer, hymn, collection, special music, sermon, and benediction, followed by the exodus. What is it about this type of service that warrants use of the word "worship"? One of the authors asked this question for many years and finally came to the conclusion that what most of us call worship is nothing more than a *lecture with hymns!* This seems to be a far cry from the practices of the Old Testament saints:

> Sing a new song to the Lord telling about his mighty deeds! For he has won a mighty victory by his power and holiness. He has announced this victory and revealed it to every nation by fulfilling his promise to be kind to Israel. The whole earth has seen God's salvation of his people. That is why the earth breaks out in praise to God, and sings for utter joy! . . . Make a joyful symphony before the Lord, the King! . . . Let the earth and all those living on it shout, "Glory to the Lord." (from Psalm 98, *Living Bible*)

True worship was a joyous occasion of giving united praise to God, focusing on His attributes, raising one voice of adoration for His greatness. It is an occasion for the Body of Christ to communicate with God collectively and to acknowledge His deity.[1]

Most of our so-called worship services fall far short of this model. The sermon, for example, is a means of teaching, and, as was pointed out before, it is by no means certain that it deserves the central place we have given it. Why don't we be honest and say that we really are having an 11:00 A.M. hour of instruction? There is nothing wrong with that as long as we don't mix the service of praise and the service of instruction.

We wonder what might happen in the Church if the true meaning of worship were to penetrate the Sunday morning service? Perhaps joy would be contagious and a sense of the miraculous would once again pervade God's people. A dream? Perhaps. Whatever the case, worship *is* communication from God's people to Him, and its rightful function must not be ignored.

Equipped by God

God has left His Church on earth for a ministry of reconciliation, and He has equipped it to perform all its proper functions. First, the Holy Spirit is a divine presence for guidance and empowering as already was mentioned. Second, the Body of Christ is characterized by the presence of spiritual gifts. Some of the gifts itemized in the New Testament (Romans 12, Ephesians 4, and 1 Corinthians 12-14) are leadership gifts: those of teacher, evangelist, apostle, and prophet. Other gifts given for the work of ministry include miracles, healing, administration, tongues, and additional gifts that no doubt are given as the need arises. Those gifts that are particularly related to ministry in the world are evangelism, prophecy, and apostleship.

---

[1] The congregation at Circle Church in Chicago has made some interesting attempts to restore worship to this pattern of praise. See David Mains, *Full Circle* (Waco, Texas: Word Books, 1971).

It is not our purpose to develop here the significance of each gift, since this has been done adequately by others.[2] It should be stressed, however, that surveys are now beginning to disclose that most Christians either do not know their spiritual gift or do not know how to exercise it within the Body. Therefore, a fundamental ministry of cultivation of the believer is to uncover these gifts and train the believer in their use.[3]

It must also be noted that the development of gifts is virtually impossible under the conditions of Sunday-morning-only Christianity. Many of us seem to be content to let the work of the local church reside in the person of one man or a limited paid staff. Our task is only to attend, act interested, keep awake, and then leave. But let's face it, this kind of church life is nothing more than a sham. The Body of Christ is not meant to be made up of spectators.

Church organization is another inhibiting factor. Do you remember Al Cranston's comment in chapter 1 about the organization at First Church? He said it was even better than his down at the plant. First Church has established its constitution, complete with an organization chart that provides for deacons, commissions, and committees. A slate of candidates is proposed each year by a nominating committee for election to the Board of Deacons. The Deacons, in turn, appoint the membership of the various other organizational groups. The problem arises from the fact that this organization virtually precludes the recognition, development, and exercise of gifts.

In the first place, no one ever inquires whether the candidates for election meet the job description laid down in the book of Titus and elsewhere. Those who are elders or deacons really are to have spiritual oversight of the church, not just the business management function. If they don't have the gifts for this purpose, they shouldn't be elected!

Furthermore, committee slots are mostly filled by those who somehow can have their arms twisted so they will say yes. But should anyone who doesn't have the gift for teaching be permitted to teach? Should anyone administrate without

---

[2] All of the sources in footnote 3 on page 136 are helpful for this purpose.

[3] Mains, *Full Circle,* has an excellent discussion on gifts and their development.

the gift of administration? Do you see what we are driving at? *God really cannot work through an organization chart, which is just man's invention, unless it provides for a staff equipped by God to perform the functions.* No wonder we are often characterized by impotence within the Church!

Now a final word for the pastor. What precisely is his function in the Body? His biblical job description is that he has been raised up "for the equipping of the saints for the work of service, to the building up of the body of Christ" (Eph. 4:12, 13). In other words, his primary ministry is one of *cultivation.* Now, does that mean he must be a good sermon-giver to perform this function? Of course, it may help, but we should not confuse the ministry of cultivation with that of giving the Sunday morning sermon!

Also, the role of the pastor is one of serving as the "playing coach." Others are to do the work. Yet, many pastors want to keep their hands on the reigns, partly out of fear that the work won't be done well if they don't do it. This kind of an attitude, however, violates the biblical mandate. The role of the pastor is not one of getting things done through people; rather, it is one of *developing* people into men and women of God. A focus on *using people* in the program of the church is a vicious and nonbiblical dead end.

First Church is in an effectiveness crisis in large part because its very organization tends to head it in nonbiblical directions. The development of gifts, if it takes place at all, is only secondary. Tom Bartlett contributes to the problem by taking more authority and responsibility than he would if he were taking his God-given job description seriously. The Church will continue in its stage of relative impotence until these facts are recognized and serious steps taken to insure, first, that everyone is helped to find his gifts and, second, that the ministry of the Church falls to those who have been equipped by God for these purposes.

Ministering to Each Other

The book of Acts unfolds an exciting story of the church of the first century. All things were mutually shared, deep intimate fellowship was sought, and Christians developed a true sense of community that was characterized by love and acceptance. What about the church of today?

Most of us recognize the importance of fellowship. What we mean by this, however, is often a far cry from the New Testament pattern. We seem to have fallen into a non-demanding social relationship and use it as the standard. What has happened to that kind of love within the Church whereby we would "lay down our lives for the brethren" (1 John 3:16)? Ray Stedman has issued a prophetic warning:

> Jesus said the church is his body, that he is the life of the body. "There is one body and one Spirit, just as you were called to the one hope that belongs to your call, one Lord, one faith, one baptism, one God and Father of us all, who is above all and through all and in all." But in many places today it seems the life has gone out of the body. In the early church all Christians were intimately and actively involved in the vibrant life of the body. Their witness to unbelievers coupled with their deep love for each other rocked the Roman world. And it must be so again.[4]

This all-important ministry of true love within the Church is once again receiving the attention it deserves. There is no question that what is now known as the *body-life movement* is bringing a revolution. Masks are coming off and Christians are rediscovering the meaning of agape love. Small groups are springing up everywhere for the purpose of discovery and exercise of gifts, prayer, praise, mutual edification, and serious Bible study. Opportunity is given for the Holy Spirit to work freely — to teach, to heal, to work miracles. Church discipline is exercised where needed, and this performs the long-neglected but vitally needed role of demanding that Christians truly live for Christ.

Ministering to the World

As the individual believer finds his "place to stand" through

---

4 Ray C. Stedman, *Body Life* (Glendale, California: Regal Books, 1972).

small groups and through an understanding of how to exercise God-given gifts, a new vitality of outreach emerges. True evangelism is the overflow of a God-enriched life, and the entire body engages, to one degree or another, in sharing the Good News through lifestyle, deeds, and words. In addition, there is healthy recognition that Christ was concerned also for the physical and other nonspiritual needs of man. Thus, the Church is characterized by a full-orbed ministry following the example of Christ, and its presence will be felt in a community.

A Lifestyle of Obedience

The biblical Church has no benches on the sidelines of its playing field. The believer does not really have the option of moving to the sidelines in disobedience. John says, "By this we know that we have come to know Him, if we keep His commandments" (1 John 2:3). Although everyone fails, God demands a heart attitude of willingness to please Him through thoughts and actions. Anything less than this is churchianity, not Christianity.

Reproduction

Finally, the Church will be characterized by reproduction. Individual members, of course, will reproduce their lives in others along the lines discussed in previous chapters. But there is another significant dimension of reproduction — the establishment of new congregations through proclamation and persuasion. As Snyder points out, normal growth comes by the division of cells, not by the unlimited expansion of existing cells.[5] Body life becomes impossible in a congregation with thousands of members, so the objective should be to create new smaller cells as part of the overall larger organism. It is a demonstrated principle of church growth that Christianity

---

[5] Howard A. Snyder, "The Church as God's Agent of Evangelism" in *Let the Earth Hear His Voice,* official ref. vol. of the International Congress on World Evangelization, ed. J. D. Douglas (Minneapolis: World Wide Publications, 1975), pp. 327-60.

gains in a society only to the extent that the number of existing churches is multiplied.[6] Multiplication of new congregations of believers, then, is the normal and expected output of a
healthy body. God's plan for a cell in His body does not call
for establishment of a S.M.O.T.S. group (a Secret Meeting of
the Saints).

The Dead End of Renewal

A church that fulfilled these biblical characteristics would
not fit into the woodwork of society. There would be, as Tozer
puts it, "that heavenly quality which marks the Church as a
divine thing."[7] The Church, more than anything else, should
be a model to the world of what heaven, the real kingdom
of God, is all about. It should stand far above the world and
show the awe-inspiring mystery that only the presence of God
can give. Many of our churches today are only smoking hulks
of what they once were. Trying to renew an organization with
largely man-made tools is no more possible than sewing a cloth
back together without blemish after it has been torn.

The answer cannot be found in renewal as such, because as
Larson asserts, "Renewal implies going back to an earlier and
a better day."[8] Instead, we should look forward to what is yet
to be discovered — the renaissance. The key is to strip down
to the biblical essentials and center on the task yet to be done.
We've only just begun!

THE RENAISSANCE

Now let's speculate a bit about what could happen at First
Church. The congregational analysis was the initial step for

---

[6] See, for example, Neil Braun, *Laity Mobilized: Reflections on
Church Growth in Japan and Other Lands* (Grand Rapids: Wm.
B. Eerdmans Publishing Co., 1971).

[7] A. W. Tozer, *Paths to Power* (Harrisburg, Pennsylvania:
Christian Publications, Inc., n.d.), p. 6.

[8] Bruce Larson, *The One and Only You* (Waco, Texas: Word,
1973), p. 26.

First Church on its way to renaissance. Change should *never* even be contemplated without a thorough assessment of the current situation and determination of the reasons for the problems that exist.

The church is now at a critical juncture. Either it takes these data seriously and seeks the mind of the Lord in discovering the changes He wants, or it perpetuates the effectiveness crisis by taking no action whatever. It is said that the seven last words of the church are "But we've always done it this way!" Acceptance of this latter path, of course, is much easier, but, by that choice the church loses its right to use the name "church." It becomes just an organization, an empty shell.

Tom Bartlett and his deacons are, first and foremost, men of God. They are shaken, of course, by what they found out, but their desire is to restore the church to its rightful function. Therefore, they have covenanted together to follow the Head, Jesus Christ, as He leads His Body into renaissance.

Development of an Adaptive Strategy

The great temptation now will be to borrow someone else's program. "Pastor, we need to have a Lay Institute of Evangelism." Or, "Let's start the Kennedy Plan now." "I've read about Body Life, and that's the answer." And on we go! Each of these programs has served its purpose well, but there is no guarantee that any will represent God's plan for First Church. First Church must develop its *own* strategy, borrowing from others only if their ideas will meet clearly demonstrated needs.

As a case in point, the Church of the Savior in Washington D.C. began one of the first coffeehouse ministries many years ago.[9] Experience has shown that it was a clear success and that the members of this church had embarked on a Spirit-led strategy. Soon, as is well known, coffeehouses sprang up everywhere as churches and Christian groups of all types hurried to jump on the bandwagon. What has been the result? All too often we have observed downright disillusionment. And this is to be expected, because it is quite likely that man borrowed

[9] Elizabeth O'Connor, *Call to Commitment* (New York: Harper & Row, 1963).

and implemented a strategy that was not God's strategy for his unique situation. We shudder to think how many of our programs fall into this category.

First Church wisely resisted the tendency to borrow. Furthermore, a temporary holding pattern was declared for all programs of the church. The leadership declared that everything must be reviewed from the perspective of restoring the missing cutting blades.

Goals. The next step was to assemble a group of concerned laymen, including most members of the Board of Deacons, to serve as a task force to review the congregational analysis and mount a new strategy. Much of the deliberation was done over a weekend.

The demonstrated needs, in order of priority, were found to be: (1) lack of witnessing, (2) lack of oneness within the Body, (3) absence of Bible reading and spiritual growth, (4) absence of devotional life within the family, and (5) lack of outreach to meet the social needs of the community. After hours of deliberation and earnest prayer, the following goals were set for the next year:

1. *Witnessing*

   To have 80 percent respond "yes" to the statement "I feel able to talk confidently with a non-Christian about faith in Jesus Christ."

   To begin at least one form of outreach (Bible study or whatever) in every neighborhood (defined as an area of two square blocks) within the boundaries of the area served by the church.

   To reach 150 decisions for Jesus Christ through the witness of the members and to have 100 of these new Christians unite in membership with the church.

2. *Oneness within the Body*

   To have 80 percent respond "yes" to the statement "There is a positive spirit of oneness in our congregation."

   To stimulate understanding of spiritual gifts so that 60 percent could respond "yes" to the statement "I am meaningfully involved in the life of our church through use of my spiritual gifts."

To have 75 percent respond "yes" to the statement "I have close friends in this church with whom I share personal feelings and concerns."

3. *Devotional life in the family*

   To motivate 75 percent to respond "yes" to the statement "Praying together as a family is part of our home life."

4. *Bible reading*

   To motivate 90 percent to respond "yes" to the statement "I take time for personal Bible reading at least three times a week."

5. *Meeting social needs*

   To motivate 60 percent to respond "yes" to the statement "I am actively involved in meeting the social-concern needs of my neighborhood and community (lack of food or clothing, drug addiction, etc.).

Obviously some of these goals may be overly ambitious and not attainable within the time period of one year. Yet, it is probably best to err in this direction, because the church certainly has not been characterized by great vision in recent years. If our best efforts have been put forth, it is no calamity if the goal is not reached. At least we are aiming at *something*. The value of this goal statement is that it provides concrete guidance for strategy.

The Program. During their weekend meeting the analysis group set up a series of smaller task forces to determine the program in each of the five areas of priority. Once again, care was taken to involve laymen from all corners of the church. Their mandate was to meet, brainstorm, pray, and report back to the analysis group in one month with a recommended program. The larger body would then deliberate on the recommendations and forward them, with modification if necessary, to the Board of Deacons for their assessment and implementation.

Let's take a look at what happened in the meetings of the "witnessing task force." It was composed of eight members, ranging in age from fifteen to sixty-four, and it had equal numbers of men and women. All members functioned as *equals,* each contributing in accordance with his or her insight and gift. The first two meetings were largely freewheeling discussion. Sometimes the give and take became hilarious. After all, shouldn't church business also be fun? But there were also some good times in prayer, because everyone realized that the task of the group was to find the mind of the Lord and to arrive at His program. A number of plans used by others were evaluated, and this was the final recommendation:

1. Hold another evangelistic training institute for all who now say that they do not feel able to talk confidently with a non-Christian about faith in Jesus Christ.

2. Start a series of weekly visitations, mostly with visitors to church or others who have demonstrated interest (These should not be cold calls, given the skepticism in the community about Christianity). Callers will go two-by-two, with one member of each pair being experienced in personal evangelism.

3. Evaluate the spiritual situation in each neighborhood and identify and train two couples in each to start a series of neighborhood friendship coffees and meetings. The goal is not to begin with a Bible study but to initiate such studies if there is interest shown. The purpose is to get to know people first and assess their spiritual status.

4. A Christian cell group will be started at the high school with members from First Church and elsewhere. Its purpose will be to build a concerned body who will then mount various forms of evangelistic outreach to their friends. In this year the only intent is to form the group and begin training them.

This plan was well received by the larger group when it was presented one month later. The Board of Deacons also responded positively and asked openly in the church who would like to be a part of the "witness module." In other words, they asked God to raise up a group of persons who would implement the plan under their direction. Interest was shown by fourteen people who began meeting weekly to get things moving. And a surprising thing happened in this group: it soon became a functioning cell in the body of Christ. As members came to know each other, there was growing interest in bearing one another's burden, and the spiritual vitality of all who were involved jumped remarkably.

Space limitations preclude detailed evaluation of the remainder of the program, but one of the most exciting outputs was formation of cell groups in the various geographical areas served by the church. Each had an "undershepherd" who assumed responsibility for the spiritual welfare of the others. Gradually many of these groups began to meet regularly, and body life, in the sense discussed earlier, slowly became a reality.

Restoration of the Laity. Do you notice what is happening here? The laity, the people of God, are beginning to function as a unit. Little has been said about Tom Bartlett and his staff. This is because Tom, in particular, assumed his rightful place among the laity. There is nothing in the Word of God that would elevate him to unusual status. This is not to say that his gift of being pastor-teacher was downgraded. Far from it!

Tom truly started to become the playing coach. He was involved with others in setting the goals and in their implementation. Often he played the key role in providing training, and his effectiveness as a Bible teacher grew.

Something also began to happen on Sunday morning. Tom is no longer so concerned about his sermon. Oftentimes worship services have an element of spontaneity as opportunity is given for praise and sharing of needs. On numerous occasions other laymen have been given opportunity to speak. Much to his surprise, Tom has discovered that he has not lost leadership in any way. Rather, he is now exercising the true intent of leadership — to develop other people.

God's Organization. Three members of the Board of Deacons began to become very uncomfortable with their new role. Finally it became obvious that none of the three possessed the gifts required to give leadership in shepherding the flock. After much prayer, three others were nominated and elected in their place. No longer does this Board meet only once a month. Each deacon now is serving as an undershepherd in the neighborhoods.

The old committee structure also has been replaced with a

series of modules. The witnessing module is just one example. The members were helped to find their gifts and encouraged to unite with others with the same gift to spearhead appropriate ministry.

The Training Program. Christian education now has taken on a new dimension. Sunday school classes continue, but there now is a wide series of electives to appeal to varied interests and needs. Probably of greatest significance is the development of a plan for family education in which parents are trained in methods of the Christian nurture of their children. Also, new believers are immediately enrolled in a discipleship program that builds the doctrinal foundation, discovers gifts, and equips them to function effectively in the total life of the church.

Cooperation With the Mobilized Body. Finally, First Church has recognized that God's ministry of reconciliation in Rollingwood cannot be carried out by one church alone. Tom has sought interaction with his pastoral colleagues, and there is now a move afoot to mount a community outreach along the lines discussed in chapter 6.

First Church has not fallen victim to a form of separation that has no biblical foundation. Christians are admonished to be separate from the world in the sense that they are not to adopt its standards as theirs. But it is quite another thing for us to use this command in such a way that we separate ourselves from those who do not dot their theological "i's" or cross their theological "t's" in the same way we do. Some in the evangelical camp have become militantly separatistic, even to the point of continually attacking their brothers of different persuasions. Assuring that we all share the historic creeds of the Church, this type of separatism is not an expression of Christian love. As John points out, "Every one who hates his brother is a murderer; and you know that no murderer has eternal life abiding in him" (1 John 3:15). It's time we recognize militant separatism for what it is — sin!

The Results

First Church must now execute its new program for a year

or so and then begin once again with another congregational and community analysis, asking the very same questions about community needs and the needs within the congregation. The effects will be quite obvious, and the basis thus is established for the plan of the following year.

The renaissance will not occur overnight. Rather, it is gradual and is manifested as individuals themselves become renewed. The steps taken by this church, however, are those that are needed to reverse the effectiveness crisis. The adaptive strategy following the leadership of the Holy Spirit is by no means easy. There are inevitable ups and downs, but there is that quality of joy that cannot come unless the Body of Christ functions as intended.

A Word for the Parachurch Organization

Much that has been said here applies equally to the strategy of a mission society, a broadcaster, a publisher, or any other kind of agency that works alongside the church. They too must follow a Spirit-led adaptive strategy based on more than experience and intuition. Furthermore, the burden is on them to demonstrate that functions are contributing to the total ministry of the church. We would echo Snyder's warning that there is no divine permanence attached to the parachurch organization.[10] Undoubtedly, some of these agencies have outlived their usefulness. To each parachurch organization we would ask, "What evidence can you provide that those cutting blades are in place and working?"

---

[10] Snyder, "The Church as God's Agent of Evangelism."

10

Restoring the Missing
Cutting Blades

We began with the question, "What's gone wrong with the harvest?" The problem clearly does not lie in a total lack of harvest equipment, because there is an abundance of most of that! The real issue is the missing cutting blades. First, we need *a Spirit-led research-based strategy to reach people with the Good News and to build them in the faith as they grow to spiritual maturity.* Equally important, this strategy must be *designed and implemented by a properly functioning Body of Christ.*

So here you have it — the keys are to be found in the strategy and function of the Church. In many ways, much of what we have said must be painfully obvious, because most of it certainly represents common sense. Yet the obvious all too easily becomes lost, almost in the same manner as when we look at the forest we fail to see the trees. Our purpose has been to provide a "second touch" — to look at the familiar from some new perspectives and to provide some solid answers to the challenges the Church now faces.

THE IMPERATIVES FOR TODAY

Now, where do we go from here? What must be done to put those cutting blades back in place? It is necessary to review and to bring out the major generalizations from the preceding pages, and it is our prayer that these will prove useful as guidelines for any church or parachurch organization that takes its biblical mandate seriously.

Declare a Moratorium on Program Orientation

Program orientation, as you will recall, arises when a strategy decision is made on the basis of what the decision-maker thinks *ought to be* rather than on the basis of objective evidence about the circumstances to be faced. Frequently this results in a wrong decision being made in the first place, but, even more seriously, it leads to the continuation of a program long after its effectiveness has ceased. Often the decision is made simply by borrowing what has worked for "the other guy."

It almost seems as if we expect *people to adapt* to the programs of the church or the parachurch organization. The fact is that people are under no obligation to do so, and it is a complete abbrogation of biblical principles to maintain such an orientation. The Church must show that *it* is responsive to the society in which it exists. If this cannot be demonstrated, the survival of organized Christian religion is at stake. Jess Moody puts it well: "The church needs to be informed that the world isn't obligated to pay any attention to us. I am convinced that they will when we deserve to be heard. We must merit an audience."[1]

Program orientation can create a church or parachurch organization that is outwardly orthodox and prospering but is spiritually bankrupt inwardly. The emphasis becomes one of maintenance of the organization rather than ministry to the Body of Christ and to the world. The result is an easy kind of complacency in which little is demanded of, or given to, members of the congregation, and the paid staff assumes a dominating position. Those who do not conform are viewed with suspicion, and Christianity as a lifestyle becomes a very comfortable part of the milieu in which it exists.

Quite different results are achieved when decisions are made on the basis of analysis of the environment and adaptation of programs to the needs that will emerge. Change is required in a changing world!

At the same time, it must be pointed out that there are some distinct limits on change. The normal response in a business

---

[1] Jess Moody, "A Drink at Joel's Place," *Today* (August 24, 1969), p. 3.

firm, for example, is to respond to a declining market and introduce changes in its product line and advertising where necessary. It is free to do so without restrictions other than those imposed by company policy and the law.

At first glance, this appears to be a proper strategy for the Church as well. One of the leading advocates of change, Bishop Robinson, alleges that "there must be a radical recasting of the most fundamental categories of our theology — of God, of the supernatural, and of religion itself,"[2] if the Church is to avoid becoming irrelevant to all but a tiny minority. Therefore, large segments within the Church have attempted to become more relevant through a radical challenge to the authority of the Scriptures and abandonment of many long-standing doctrines, especially those pertaining to the return of the Lord, the final judgment, and salvation.

A striving for relevancy, of course, is appropriate, and it is by no means a twentieth century phenomenon. John Wesley was used by the Spirit to help institute a revival that swept England, transformed lives, and brought about dramatic social reform. In the strictest sense, however, Wesley and other reformers[3] proceeded in a manner exactly the opposite to that advocated by Robinson and other present-day radical theologians. Their effectiveness resulted from a return to the precepts of early Christianity and was based on a reaffirmation of the ultimate truth and ultimate authority of the Word of God. Christianity must adhere to its scriptural foundation if it is to be true to its stated purpose. No other institution offers a "product" that, at its very heart, claims to be based on revealed ultimate truth. To deviate from this foundation is to erect a totally different product — one that cannot legitimately be called Christianity.

Some church leaders seem to be carried away by a passion for newness as if they were deliberately instituting a policy of planned obsolescence. Once they deviate from the scriptural

---

[2] John Robinson, *Honest to God* (Philadelphia: Westminster Press, 1963), p. 7.

[3] See Richard Quebedeaux, *The Young Evangelicals* (New York: Harper & Row, 1974). However, we feel that he and other spokesmen also border on advocating change for the sake of change. This is quite different from an adaptive philosophy.

base, however, they are open to a challenge of the criteria they are using to reject the historical biblical message. At times it seems as if there are no standards whatsoever, with the result that Christianity is forced to compete with other philosophies based strictly on human wisdom and reason.

The response of laymen to "planned theological obsolescence" is decidedly negative. The late Louis Cassells made this penetrating observation about change for the sake of change:

> What I hear these modern men saying is that they're sick and tired of being told what they can't believe. They want to know what, if anything, they can believe. . . . If you persist in handing out stone where people ask for bread, they'll finally quit coming to the bakery.[4]

"If the bugle produces an indistinct sound, who will prepare himself for battle?" (1 Cor. 14:8).

Formalize the Planning Process

A Spirit-led planning process begins, proceeds, and ends with a seeking of the mind of the Lord. This almost goes without saying, but God also expects man to do his part — "We should make plans, counting on God to direct us" (Prov. 16:9, *Living Bible*). Man uses three bases for planning, all of which are guided and enriched by the Spirit: (1) experience, (2) intuition, and (3) research. All three really are necessary, but all too frequently research is considered to be irrelevant. Yet, we have shown that the planning process *demands* research if it is to be done correctly, especially in analysis of the environment and measurement of effectiveness. Research is basically a collection of any type of information useful for planning — surveys may or may not be needed!

The task of world evangelization lies before the Church. It is clear that the past methods have not fully accomplished the job. We have no choice but to take seriously our responsi-

---

[4] Louis Cassels, "The Recovery of the Positive," *Christianity Today* (April 25, 1969), pp. 3, 4.

bility of *managing the resources God has given us to accomplish His goal.* This cannot be done by going on, "business as usual."

Many, if not most, who are involved in the Church or the parachurch organization are going to require new training. Such tools as computers, statistics, sample surveys, the latest in graphics, and cable television will become commonplace. But these tools cannot be used in the hands of amateurs. At the very minimum, anyone who claims to be a professional in communication today must have a working knowledge of audience psychology and behavior, techniques of research, the fundamentals of media selection, advanced training in creative writing or message preparation, and an appreciation of updated methods in graphics and production. The secular businessman often spends as much as one month a year in executive training and development, both on and off the job. Can the Church and its leadership afford to do anything less?

Now, a word to the Christian educational institution. Some of us seem to feel that adequate training in communication has been provided if the student has learned how to prepare a polished three-point sermon (which may or may not make a polished three-point landing). The emphasis, then, is on the *message* and not on *understanding the audience* — therein lies the crucial failure! Moreover, sermon preparation is just one part of the total communication function of the Church. Our sights must be raised to comprehend the crucial role to be played by a multiple-media, multiple-church strategy.

Adoption of a New Lifestyle in the Church

Henry G. Bosch tells the interesting story of what happened when a customer in a small store discovered that the slow-moving clerk was not around one morning:

"Where's Eddie? Is he sick?"

"Nope," came the reply. "He ain't workin' here no more."

"Do you have anyone in mind for the vacancy?" inquired the customer.

"Nope! *Eddie didn't leave no vacancy!*"[5]

There are quite a few "Eddies" in most churches today. They leave, and no one even notices. Why? First, because there is no real sense of the Body of Christ in which members are involved in a functioning manner. Second, many, by their own decision, have chosen to sit on the church bench on the sidelines of the action.

God expects something quite different, as we have said in many ways earlier. Any benches in the Church today are strictly man-made, because God does not allow us that luxury. Obedience to His commands is expected.

It is not necessary to repeat what has been said before, except to make one more point. And that is that God expects us to keep our focus on *His* goals for the Body of Christ. Now that seems to be an obvious point, so why make it? The reason is that some of us take on functions that God never intended — especially straitjacketing and criticism of the leadership. "If you don't stop playin' that rock music for those kids, you won't get another dime from me." "What kind of tract is this? It doesn't even tell them how to pray to receive Christ." "If you don't stop using that modern Bible in the Sunday school, my kids aren't coming back."

Heard any of this before? You see, we are focusing on the wrong things. We must always ask just one question: Are the methods getting God's results? If not, say your piece, but don't be a critic just because you don't like something. If we truly are the Body of Christ, centering on meeting God's goals together, it is amazing how trivial differences disappear.

Return the Church to Its Biblical Roots

This, of course, was the subject of chapter 9, but let it simply be noted here that we must turn our spiritual searchlight on our programs, organizational structures, and methods to see if we are truly adhering to the biblical principles. Of particular significance is review of the organization to ascer-

---

[5] H. G. Bosch, "He Left No Vacancy," *Our Daily Bread* (May, 1974), given as the devotional for May 6, 1974.

tain that the church is manned by those who have been gifted by God to do His work. Anything less than that will only inhibit the carrying out of our intended functions.

Cooperate With Others in a Multiple-Media Strategy

Chapter 4 made the point that the ministry of proclamation and persuasion demands a cooperative strategy using *all* appropriate media. No single church or parachurch organization can do much more than the equivalent of aiming a tiny hose at a forest fire.

Some will react violently, objecting to what looks like an attempt to revive the contemporary ecumenical movement, which is gasping for life. That is not our intent for a moment. Frankly, we feel that the ecumenical movement as it has been expressed to date should be allowed to die and should be buried without a tombstone. Our convictions about maintenance of the biblical distinctives should be abundantly apparent to the reader by now.

We are pleased that God truly is at work to build a spirit of cooperation within His Church. This is not just a glib statement but results from observation based on world travels. Something exciting is happening. It seems as if God is now mobilizing the Church for one last great push. We notice wherever we go a motivation that calls for cooperation and for a Spirit-led strategy. For this reason, we are greatly encouraged about the future of the Church. We may not have many years left — who knows? — but it does seem that God is doing something totally unprecedented. From our limited human perspective, it appears that we have both the manpower and the media to finish His work in our lifetime. Are we prepared to venture out in faith, with others, in some uncharted waters?

A LAST WORD

Mark said, "And they went out and preached everywhere, while the Lord worked with them, and confirmed the word by the signs that followed (Mark 16:20). This, in a nutshell, is the work of the Church — a united body going *out,* preaching, with the Lord confirming His presence by signs and miracles. Have any miracles happened in your church lately? Why not?

It is our responsibility to release that divine power into the world today. To restate Tozer's powerful words:

> The Church must have power; she must become formidable, a moral force to be reckoned with, if she would regain her lost position of spiritual ascendancy and make her message the revolutionizing, conquering thing it once was.[6]

We lack nothing that is necessary to finish God's work. Let's get those cutting blades back in place and expect miracles!

---

[6] A. W. Tozer, *Paths to Power* (Philadelphia: Christian Publications, Inc., n.d.), p. 5.

Bibliography

BOOKS

Backstrom, C. H. and Hursh, G. D. *Survey Research*. Evanston, Illinois: Northwestern University Press, 1963.

Bayly, Joseph. *Out of My Mind*. Wheaton, Illinois: Tyndale House Publishers, 1970.

Bogart, Leo. *Strategy in Advertising*. New York: Harcourt, Brace and World, 1967.

Bower, Robert T. *Television and the Public*. New York: Holt, Rinehart and Winston, 1973.

Braun, Neil. *Laity Mobilized: Reflections on Church Growth in Japan and Other Lands*. Grand Rapids: Wm. B. Eerdmans Publishing Co., 1971.

Costas, Orlando E. *The Church and Its Mission: A Shattering Critique From the Third World*. Wheaton, Illinois: Tyndale House Publishers, 1974.

Drucker, Peter F. *The Effective Executive*. New York: Harper & Row, 1966.

Engel, James F.; Kollat, David T.; and Blackwell, Roger D. *Consumer Behavior*. rev. ed. New York: Holt, Rinehart and Winston, 1973.

Engel, James F.; Wales, Hugh G.; and Warshaw, Martin R. *Promotional Strategy*. Homewood, Illinois: Richard D. Irwin, Inc., 1975.

Gangel, Kenneth O. *Leadership for Church Education*. Chicago: Moody Press, 1970.

Girard, Robert C. *Brethren, Hang Loose*. Grand Rapids: Zondervan Publishing House, 1972.

Goodenough, Ward H. *Cooperation in Change*. New York: Russell Sage Foundation, 1963.

Larson, Bruce. *The One and Only You*. Waco, Texas: Word Books, 1973.

161

Lindsey, Hal. *The Late Great Planet Earth.* Grand Rapids: Zondervan Publishing House, 1970.

Mains, David. *Full Circle.* Waco, Texas: Word Books, 1971.

Maslow, A. H. *Motivation and Human Behavior.* rev. ed. New York: Harper & Row, 1970.

McGavran, Donald A. *How Churches Grow.* New York: Friendship Press, 1955.

————. *Understanding Church Growth.* Grand Rapids: Wm. B. Eerdmans Publishing Co., 1969.

McLuhan, Marshall and Fiore, Quentin. *The Medium Is the Message.* New York: Bantam Books, 1970.

Miller, Keith. *The Becomers.* Waco, Texas: Word Books, 1973.

Nichols, Alan, *The Communicators.* Sydney: Pilgrim Productions, Ltd., 1972.

O'Connor, Elizabeth. *Call to Commitment.* New York: Harper & Row, 1963.

Quebedeaux, Richard. *The Young Evangelicals.* New York: Harper & Row, 1974.

Raines, Robert. *New Life in the Church.* New York: Harper & Row, 1961.

Reid, Gavin. *The Gagging of God.* London: Hodder and Stoughton, 1969.

Richards, Lawrence O. *A New Face for the Church.* Grand Rapids: Zondervan Publishing House, 1970.

Robinson, John. *Honest to God.* Philadelphia: Westminster Press, 1963.

Rogers, Everett M. and Shoemaker, F. Floyd. *Communication of Innovations.* New York: Free Press, 1971.

Stedman, Ray E. *Body Life.* Glendale, California: Regal Books, 1972.

Toffler, Alvin. *Future Shock.* New York: Random House, 1970.

Tozer, A. W. *Paths to Power.* Philadelphia: Christian Publications, Inc., n.d.

Trueblood, Elton. *A Place to Stand.* New York: Harper & Row, 1969.

————. *The Incendiary Fellowship.* New York: Harper & Row, 1967.

Wagner, C. Peter. *Frontiers in Missionary Strategy.* Chicago: Moody Press, 1971.

————. *Look Out! The Pentecostals Are Coming.* Carol Stream, Illinois: Creation House, 1973.

Wish, J. R. and Gamble, S. H., eds. *Marketing and Social Issues.* New York: John Wiley & Sons, 1971.

Wuest, Kenneth S. *Studies in the Vocabulary.* Grand Rapids: Wm. B. Eerdmans Publishing Co., 1945.

PERIODICALS

Articles on cable television. *Religious Broadcasting* (April-May, 1974).

Cassels, Louis. "The Recovery of the Positive." *Christianity Today* (April 25, 1969).

Bosch, H. G. "He Left No Vacancy." *Our Daily Bread* (May, 1974).

Chin, T. G. N. "New Product Success and Failures — How to Detect Them in Advance." *Advertising Age* (September 24, 1973).

Kraft, Charles. "God's Model for Cross-Cultural Communication: The Incarnation." *Evangelical Missions Quarterly,* 1 (1973):205-16.

————. "Dynamic Equivalence Churches: An Ethnotheological Approach to Indigeneity." *Missiology,* 1 (1973):39-57.

————. "Christian Conversion As a Dynamic Process." *International Christian Broadcasters Bulletin* (Second Quarter, 1974).

Miller, Donald. "How to Publish in Nigeria for Nominal Christians in Churches." Mimeographed report, Sudan Interior Mission Communication Center, May, 1973.

Moody, Jess. "A Drink at Joel's Place." *Today* (August 24, 1969).

"Radio Reach Is Everywhere — Homes, Autos, Outdoors."
  Advertising Age (November 21, 1973).
Sorensen, Wanda. "A Way of Life for Dynamic Church
  Growth: The Way of Life Plan." *Worldwide Impact*
  (May, 1974).

Index